HEARING THE WORD SERIES

# Lutheran Perspectives on BIBLICAL INTERPRETATION

The 2009 Hein-Fry Lectures
Series XIX

Laurie Jungling, editor

Lutheran University Press
Minneapolis, Minnesota

# Lutheran Perspectives on Biblical Interpretation

HEARING THE WORD SERIES
The 2009 Hein-Fry Lectures • Series XIX

Laurie Jungling, editor

Copyright 2010 Lutheran University Press, an imprint of 1517 Media. All rights reserved.

Library of Congress Cataloging-in Publication data
    Library of Congress Cataloging-in-Publication Data

    Lutheran perspectives on biblical interpretation : the 2009 Hein-Fry lectures / Laurie Jungling, editor.
        p. cm. -- (Hearing the Word series. Series XIX)
    ISBN-13: 978-1-932688-56-6 (alk. paper)
    ISBN-10: 1-932688-56-0 (alk. paper)
    eISBN: 978-1-942304-67-8
    1. Bible--Hermeneutics. 2. Evangelical Lutheran Church in America–Doctrines. I. Jungling, Laurie. II. Title: Hein-Fry lectures.
    BS47.L98 2010
    220.601--dc22
                                                        2010044012

# Table of Contents

Foreword .................................................................................... 5

Preface ....................................................................................... 7

Introduction ............................................................................... 9
    Richard A. Jensen

Interpreting the Bible Lutheranly:
Between the Undertow and a Tsunami ................................... 11
    Craig L. Nessan

Law and Gospel and the Interpretation of Scripture ............... 36
    Mark Allan Powell

Interpret Boldly: Lutherans Reading the Bible ........................ 59
    Esther Menn

Does this Text Have a Future?
Eschatology in Lutheran Biblical Interpretation ..................... 89
    Mary Hinkle Shore

*Sensus Literalis*: Another View on Luther's Legacy
and Modern Readers of the Bible ........................................... 106
    Steed Vernyl Davidson

The Lecturers ........................................................................... 128

# Foreword

## The Hein-Fry Lecture Series

The annual Hein-Fry Lecture Series is the premier endowed theological lecture series of the Evangelical Lutheran Church in America (ELCA). For the annual series, the governing committee identifies lively, pressing theological issues facing the church. The lectures, traditionally delivered at the eight ELCA seminaries, are free and open to the public.

The goals of the lecture series are to:

- foster original scholarship,
- encourage broad dialogue throughout the church on a theological topic, and
- give seminary faculty, students, clergy, church leaders, and other interested persons access to leading theologians.

The Hein Fry Lecture Series grows out of prestigious traditions dating back more than fifty years in the histories of the ELCA predecessor church bodies.

The Hein Lectures were first held at the American Lutheran Church seminary in Columbus, Ohio. After 1960 the Hein Seminary Lectures were held each year at the four seminaries of The American Lutheran Church. The Fry Lectures continue and expand on the series known as Knubel-Miller-Greever Lectures, which were held at various seminaries and other locations of the Lutheran Church in America.

The Hein-Fry Lecture Series is unique in that it addresses all the seminary communities within a major American denomination. This gives the series great potential for engaging both the current theological leadership and a generation of ministerial candidates in discussion of a focused theological issue.

The series is coordinated by the Vocation and Education unit of the Evangelical Lutheran Church in America. Lecture topics, speakers, and schedules are set by the Hein-Fry Lecture Series Governing Committee:

Rev. Jessica Crist
> Northern Rockies Institute of Theology, Great Falls, Montana

Dr. Duane Larson
> Wartburg Theological Seminary, Dubuque, Iowa

Bishop Robert Hofstad
> Southwestern Washington Synod, Tacoma, Washington

Dean Donald Huber
> Trinity Lutheran Seminary, Columbus, Ohio

Rev. Jana Schofield
> Mount Carmel Lutheran Church, San Luis Obispo, California

Ms. Carolyn Wright
> Program Committee, ELCA Vocation and Education, Fargo, North Dakota

Rev. Dr. Jonathan P. Strandjord
> Director of Theological Education, ELCA Vocation and Education, Chicago, Illinois

Rev. Laurie Jungling, Ph.D.
> Hein-Fry Lecture Series Administrator, ELCA Vocation and Education, Great Falls, Montana

# Preface

**Hearing the Word!**

In August 2007, the Churchwide Assembly of the Evangelical Lutheran Church in America approved a major initiative entitled Book of Faith: Lutherans Read the Bible. This initiative has the goal of "raising to a new level this church's individual and collective engagement with the Bible and its teaching, yielding greater biblical fluency and a more profound appreciation of Lutheran principles and approaches for the use of Scripture." In a desire to participate in the advancement of the ELCA's Book of Faith initiative, the Hein-Fry Governing Committee developed a three-year sequence for the Hein-Fry Lectures entitled "Hearing the Word."

The specific topics for this three-year sequence are:

- 2009 – "Hearing the Word: Lutheran Perspectives on Biblical Interpretation"
- 2010 – "Hearing the Word: Teaching the Bible in the Parish (and Beyond)"
- 2011 – "Hearing the Word: Lutherans Read the Bible with the Ecumenical World"

**"So faith comes from what is heard, and what is heard comes through the word of Christ" (Romans 10:17).**

The Hein-Fry lecture topic for 2009 was "Hearing the Word: Lutheran Perspectives on Biblical Interpretation." This theme was chosen in order to engage the crucial conversation facing the ELCA concerning various Lutheran approaches to Scripture and what resources and challenges those approaches bring to diverse North American contexts. The hope for these lectures is that they raise awareness about the various ways the Lutheran church has traditionally interpreted the Bible as well as explore a mixture of contemporary approaches to scriptural interpretation that Lutherans might offer today. Five scholars affiliated with the ELCA were invited to offer lectures out of their particular perspectives and scholarship. Each lecturer traveled to three sites where he or she delivered major presentations exploring important and innovative Lutheran perspectives on biblical interpretation, making a case for the promise of one, some, or even all of them. At most of the sites, a local respondent reflected in a second session on the traveling lecturer's presentation in light of its relevance to the regional context. A third session was designed to bring the two speakers into conversation with each other and the audience.

The Hein-Fry lectures for 2009 took place between February and April 2009. In order to expand the reach of this important conversation, the committee elected to bring the lectures to seven sites in addition to the eight ELCA seminaries traditionally visited. These new sites included four ELCA-affiliated colleges and three congregational forums in areas of the country not easily served by the eight seminaries. Thus, the Hein-Fry lectures were delivered at a total of fifteen sites in 2009.

# Introduction

The essays in this book are the 2009 Hein-Fry Lectures delivered at fifteen locations throughout the Evangelical Lutheran Church in America as an adjunct to the systematic five-year program for the whole church called the Book of Faith Initiative. The purpose of the initiative is to lead members of the ELCA into an ever deeper grasp of the Holy Scriptures as the source and norm of Christian faith. The lectures speak to the matter of biblical interpretation and make a helpful contribution to the life of the church.

The opening lecture is by Craig L. Nessan, theological professor at Wartburg Theological Seminary. His presentation is entitled "Interpreting the Bible Lutheranly: Between the Undertow and a Tsunami." Prof. Nessan locates his remarks in the context of an American scene where a postmodern approach to Scripture leads to an entirely subjective reading of Scripture and a literalistic approach to Scripture where the meaning of texts is objective and "over-determined." Nessan tries to navigate an approach to Scripture that moves "between the undertow of subjectivity . . . and the tsunami of objectivity demanded in biblical literalism."

His lecture, therefore, offers navigational instructions for interpreting the Bible "Lutheranly." He deals with eight concepts from Martin Luther which he offers as a Lutheran hermeneutic valid in our time. He deals with these eight concepts in a clear, concise, and helpful manner. This is as good an explanation of Luther's hermeneutical principles as I have ever encountered.

The second lecture is by Mark Allan Powell, professor of New Testament at Trinity Lutheran Seminary. He investigates in further detail one of Nessan's points: Law and Gospel. Powell includes a helpful chart which summarizes his take on Law and Gospel as a Lutheran hermeneutical principle. What is most useful in his article is his creative dealing with the concept of the "third use of the law" in Lutheran theology. He also applies this concept to the task of preaching Law and Gospel. I have rarely encountered a more helpful article in understanding the concepts of Law and Gospel in the preaching task.

Lecture three is by Esther Menn, an Old Testament professor at the Lutheran School of Theology at Chicago. Her presentation is titled "Interpret Boldly: Lutherans Reading the Bible." In her article she uses methods of interpretation which go beyond strict Lutheran principles, but she also helps us to see what might be distinctive about a Lutheran approach to a text from 2 Kings 5:1-19. She specializes in feminist insights to this text. I honestly do not know when I have read a more enlightening exegetical article than this! Her exegesis of the text opens all kinds of new possibilities in biblical interpretation. I was enthralled.

Fourth is a lecture by Mary Hinkle Shore, professor of New Testament at Luther Theological Seminary. Her article is titled "Does This Text Have a Future? Eschatology in Lutheran Biblical Interpretation." She asks a basic question: "How are texts usable in the congregation?" She approaches this topic with three theses for understanding the Bible: 1) Scripture is an extended story in which we play a part. 2) The Bible has a particular main character. 3) The ending of the story keeps breaking into the middle of life. Jesus is, of course, the ending of the story that keeps appearing in the middle of our lives even today. She gives several examples of her exegetical reading to help us grasp her thesis.

Fifth, is a lecture by Steed Vernyl Davidson, professor of Old Testament at Pacific Lutheran Theological Seminary. The title of his lecture is: "*Sensus Literalis*: Another View on Luther's Legacy and Modern Readers of the Bible." This article is a broadly comprehensive and somewhat technical review of what a literal reading of Scripture has looked like from the New Testament times until the present. He discusses Luther's literal reading of the Bible in this broad historical context. One point he makes about Luther is that, because he saw Christ as the Word who comes with the word, then faith stands as the goal of Scriptures and their reading. Reading the Bible literally is to be engaged in an existential encounter with Christ, who is king of Scripture.

These articles offer much food for thought as we seek to grasp the meaning of the Book of Faith in our time. I commend them to you.

Richard A. Jensen
Lutheran School of Theology at Chicago, *emeritus*.

# Interpreting the Bible Lutheranly
*Between the Undertow and a Tsunami*[1]

Craig L. Nessan
*Wartburg Theological Seminary*

Like the ocean, the Holy Bible is vast, mysterious, and rich with unexplored depths. Consisting of thirty-nine Old Testament writings and twenty-seven New Testament books, the various genres of literature are like ecological niches within the whole, each worthy of detailed attention. At the same time, the Bible strangely continues to speak to each new generation with inexplicable power—God's Word transcending the particularities of space and time. Nevertheless, we find ourselves in a time when many Christians have lost fascination with this holy writing, and biblical illiteracy is on the increase. The culture of which we are a part is rapidly losing even cursory familiarity with the biblical narratives.

For the next three years, the Hein-Fry lecture series will be devoted to the recovery of distinctively Lutheran approaches to reading and appropriating the Bible for the life of the church. This emphasis is an important part of the Evangelical Lutheran Church in America's five-year collaborative initiative called Book of Faith: Lutherans Read the Bible.[2] I am grateful for the invitation to be counted among the lecturers assisting the church to understand and appreciate the treasure which is ours as Lutheran interpreters of the Bible. This is not to diminish the particular contributions of others to the task of biblical interpretation. In fact, we as Lutherans are beneficiaries of a broad ecumenical consortium of scholarship devoted to the study and interpretation of Scripture, and we owe a tremendous debt to those of other traditions as we explore some distinctive hermeneutical and theological insights that derive from our own peculiar history and confessional commitments. It is important to remember how much we owe to others as readers of the Bible, even as we turn to our assigned theme, "Hearing the Word: Lutheran Perspectives on Biblical Interpretation."

## Between the Undertow and a Tsunami

How do we gain our bearings for articulating some particularly Lutheran perspectives on biblical interpretation today? Let us begin by locating ourselves on the nautical map amid two inexorable forces that affect how we undertake this voyage. First, we need to recognize the mighty undertow[3] of certain postmodern approaches to Scripture, such as reader-response criticism or deconstruction, both of which forefront human subjectivity in the process of interpretation. As a school of literary criticism, reader-response approaches focus intently on the reader and the reader's idiosyncratic "experience" of a written text.[4] This can be contrasted with those approaches that pay strict attention to the author, content, and form of a work. The primary actor in the interpretation of a text becomes the reader, who lends the text meaning through an act of creative imagination. Reading is a performing art in which each reader creates his or her own unique, text-related performance. The text means what it means to "me."

Deconstruction in a different way also shifts attention to human subjectivity in the process of interpretation.[5] Committed to the premise that language is incapable of communicating anything about what "is," deconstruction emphasizes how language is limited to making comparisons between things and pointing out differences. Deconstruction approaches texts with suspicion about how authors—wittingly or not—disguise metaphysical assumptions which serve their own privileges through what they write. Deconstruction is a strategy of interpretation for disclosing inherent contradictions and unmasking false claims. Similar to reader-response criticism, deconstruction shifts the focus from content to human subjectivity, this time not in celebration of human creativity as expressed in the act of reading but in suspicion of the unwarranted assumptions and self-interest hidden in texts.

Both reader-response criticism and deconstruction are approaches in which the meanings of texts are "under-determined." That is, we approach texts not in order to discover what is being talked about but rather to explore the subjectivity of the one who is doing the talking.

Each of these approaches reflects in its own way the hyper-individualism of much postmodernism. All claims for shared meaning communicated through writing and every sign of meta-narrative is subject to the power of an undertow which sucks us under the waves and drowns all hint of universal significance, including (especially?) theological claims about God and God's activity.

A second overwhelming force with which we must contend as we seek to interpret the Bible is literalism.[6] Biblical literalism as an oceanic force emerged in the nineteenth century and was strengthened by the development of fundamentalism in the early twentieth century. Since that time biblical literalism has been increasing in influence and, like a tsunami, washing away the nuance and complexity of other modes of interpretation. Literalism has been fostered among many church members (including Lutherans) through its prominence in the media (TV evangelists) and much "Christian" literature. Literalism famously insists on the historical occurrence of many biblical statements, for example, a six-day creation or 40 day flood. Such belief leads literalists to oppose the theory of evolution as conflicting with biblical creationism and to understand the apocalyptic symbols of Daniel and Revelation as predictive of events that will actually take place in the end times. While literalism does allow for metaphor and parable in certain Scripture passages, its preference is always for the literal happening of the events described. Biblical literalism is grounded upon belief in the inerrancy of the Bible, guided by the conviction that the original autographs (that is, manuscripts) were inspired by God in such a way as to make them free from error of every kind.

If the meaning of texts is under-determined in many postmodern approaches to the Bible, it is even more the case that the meaning of texts is typically "over-determined" by biblical literalism. This means that clearly defined and formulated theological commitments about the nature of Scripture and divine truth predetermine the meaning of particular Bible passages. These commitments were codified in the "five fundamentals" (which gave name to fundamentalism): the inerrancy of Scripture, the virgin birth and deity of Jesus, the doctrine of substitutionary atonement, the bodily resurrection of Jesus, and the pre-millennial second coming of Christ. As this listing demonstrates, fundamentalist theology concentrates on "propositional revelation," the doctrines and teachings which God has revealed to humanity in the Bible which the faithful are expected to believe and defend. It is a highly rational approach to Christian faith. Based on its theological convictions about the nature of Scripture, fundamentalism rejects all forms of "higher criticism" which investigate the origins, sources, and historical development of the biblical books in favor of a doctrine of plenary inspiration by God to the biblical writers.[7] It is important for us to recognize how the theological commitments of fundamentalism predetermine what the Bible "must" say.

As Lutherans seek to chart a course through the ocean of God's Word in Scripture, we must navigate today between the undertow of subjectivity found in many postmodern approaches and the tsunami of objectivity demanded in biblical literalism. How can we steer between an under-determination of meaning on the one side and the over-determination of meaning on the other? I will offer in this lecture eight navigational instructions for interpreting the Bible Lutheranly. These instructions are informed by the Lutheran confessional tradition and developed in conversation with key insights from recent hermeneutical theory. This map can help us chart a course for renewing the interpretation of the Bible in the Lutheran church in our time.

### 1. God speaks! (*Deus dixit*)

"In the beginning when God created the heavens and the earth, the earth was a formless void and darkness covered the face of the waters, while the spirit of God swept over the face of the waters. Then God said, "Let there be..." [Gen 1: 1-3]. God speaks and it happens! This is at the heart of the first creation story. The spirit enlivens God's Word and things come into being: light, sky, earth and vegetation, the heavens, creatures of sea and sky, animals of the land, and even human beings. Six days of creation. God speaks and creation happens!

The internal evidence of Scripture to the efficaciousness of God's Word is plentiful. Perhaps the most frequently cited (and misunderstood?) text about the inspiration of Scripture is 2 Timothy 3:16-17: "All scripture is inspired by God and is useful for teaching, for reproof, for correction, and for training in righteousness, so that everyone who belongs to God may be proficient, equipped for every good work." Notice how the force of this text is directed at what inspired Scripture has the power to do—teach, reprove, correct, train—what Scripture does to those who hear. So where does the inspiration of Scripture lie? Is inspiration rightly understood as the dictation of the words by God to the original *amanuensis*? Is inspiration manifested in the pages of a book? The doctrine of verbal inspiration (and its corollary, inerrancy) arises at the originating fissure from whence the tsunami of literalism is generated. On the other side, is inspiration confined to what the reader makes (or does not make) of a biblical text? Is every classical text just as inspired as a biblical text? The undertow of certain postmodern readings would make the meaning of divine inspiration vacuous.

Here (as elsewhere) I propose an alternative view which might be called "dynamic inspiration."[8] God remains ever sovereign over the event of inspiration; God does not deposit inspiration in what becomes a manual for our use in codifying divine truths. Instead, inspiration is an event that God created then and God creates ever anew at the confluence of the proclamation of Scripture, our hearing, and the arrival of the Holy Spirit. Inspiration is a verb, not a noun. It is an event that God brings to pass in the reading, teaching, and preaching of God's Word by the power of the Spirit. The church must continually implore God to send the Spirit to our attempts to interpret the Word—what Yves Congar described as an ongoing *epiclesis*.[9] We pray that God continues to speak to us through this Word as to people of old: "Come, Holy Spirit!"

This dynamic understanding of inspiration, inspiration as event, is core to Luther's own view of God acting through the Word. Luther distinguished between the outer Word and the inner Word. The outer Word is Scripture, while the inner Word is "God's own voice by his Spirit. Without this inner Word of God the outward Word remains a letter, the word of man."[10] Regin Prenter articulated well Luther's own dynamic view of the event of inspiration:

> When we hear the Word of the Scripture, we are compelled to wait on the Spirit of God. It is God who has the Scripture in his hand. If God does not infuse his Spirit the hearer of the Word is not different from the deaf man. No one can rightly understand the Word of God unless he receives it directly from the Holy Spirit."[11]

Luther, in contrast to his scholastic opponents, refused to understand the inspiration of the Word *ex opere operato* (that is, as automatic or, some would say, magical). Likewise, Luther's view differs from every concept of verbal inspiration. Luther's understanding of inspiration is "realistic" and dynamic, not an "idealistic" view in which "the revelation is at the mercy of the one who has the means of grace."[12] Hearers of the Word must await (or even anticipate) God's ever new act of bringing Spirit to the Word in our presence.

If the Bible itself is replete with evidence internal to Scripture about the efficacy of God speaking through the Word, is there any evidence external to the Bible for the claim that "God speaks" through the Word? The only solid external evidence for the claim that God speaks through Scripture is the existence of believers themselves. In every generation the church has testified to the power of God's Word giving her life. God continues to engender and foster faith in the lives of those "who hear the word of God and obey it" (Luke 11: 28). The very existence of the church as a community gathered around the Word of God testifies to the reality that God continues to speak through the Bible and its proclamation.

## 2. The finite bears the infinite (*Finiti capax infiniti*)

While it was in controversy over the nature of Christ's presence in the Lord's Supper that Luther most ardently defended the thesis that the finite is capable of bearing the infinite, this affirmation is consistent also with his view of the relationship between the human and the divine in Scripture. Against Zwingli, Luther insisted that God employs earthly means as bearers of Christ in the world. Christ is really present—not just spiritually or symbolically present—in the bread and wine.[13] Luther was emphatic about this truth, because at root the incarnation itself was at stake. How human was Jesus? When the Scripture says that "the Word became flesh" (John 1:14), how are we to understand the relation of the divine God to human matter? Luther's Christology insisted on the very divine presence in the fleshly humanity of Jesus Christ. Just as Jesus himself was fully human—a baby at his mother's breast, weeping at the death of his friend, suffering death by crucifixion, and lying in the tomb—so Jesus Christ's body is actually, really present in the bread of Holy Communion.

George Wolfgang Forell makes the connection between Luther's defense of the finite as bearer of the infinite in the sacrament with his understanding of the Bible:

> The implications of this emphasis upon the significance of the finite as a medium of God's revelation is clearly seen in the

conviction that the bread and the wine of Holy Communion are simultaneously the body and blood of Christ and, perhaps not as clearly to many Lutherans, that the human words of Paul and Peter are the Word of God.[14]

In some ways ahead of his time, Luther intuited the complex historical process according to which the Bible acquired its form. Therefore Luther freely employed what we have come to describe as elements of historical criticism to interpret the biblical text.

Willem Jan Kooiman describes Luther's approach:

> He was convinced that various prophetic books (as well as some epistles) were not written by the men whose names were attached to them, but were rather assembled by redactors. The book of Ecclesiastes, in his opinion, does not come from the hand of Solomon. When one of his table companions remarks that in the judgment of many the Pentateuch was not written by Moses, Luther asks, "What does it matter?" Elsewhere he gives expression to his conviction that many of the laws credited to Moses existed long before his time. . . . Nor was Luther silent about difficulties arising from a comparison of the gospels, since they do not always agree in details. The Passion history, especially, he regarded as "extremely confused" at various points.[15]

Clearly, Luther as a professor of Scripture understood that the Bible developed in a process subject to the vagaries of human authorship and redaction. Luther's own method of biblical interpretation anticipates aspects of what we have come to describe as historical criticism, that method which investigates the historical circumstances of authorship, the possible use of source material, the process of editing texts, etc.

However, at the same time that Luther opened the door to scholarly investigation of Scripture, he continued to insist that God speaks through this very human book. While holding no doctrine of verbal inspiration, Luther maintained a profound respect for the authority of the living voice of God continuing to speak through the human words of the Bible. "He was concerned about a dynamic and functional understanding of the Word of God that happens now, rather than a legalistic manipulation of a once-and-for-all inspired book."[16] Just as Christ is both true God and fully human, so the Bible is both Word of God and fully human words. Luther wrote:

> Holy Scripture possesses no external glory, attracts no attention, lacks all beauty and adornment. You can scarcely imagine that anyone would attach faith to such a divine Word, because it is without any glory or charm. Yet faith comes from this divine Word, through its inner power without any external loveliness. It is only the internal working of the Holy Spirit that causes us to place our trust in this Word of God, which is without form or comeliness.[17]

To extend our metaphor, God chooses to sail with us in a very finite, fragile vessel.

### 3. Privileging the literal sense (*Sensus literalus*)

Because of the distortions to Scripture inflicted by the interpretive authority of pope and councils, Luther insisted on the authority of Scripture alone (*sola Scriptura*). Whereas in classical medieval exegesis there developed a fourfold approach to the interpretation of Scripture, Luther gave clear priority to the literal (or "plain") sense of the text. In this fourfold medieval approach, the literal sense had been considered many times inferior to the allegorical (which pointed to the text's doctrinal importance), moral (which pointed out the text's meaning for the individual's life), or anagogical (which pointed to the text's eschatological meaning). Luther employed the literal sense of a text to regulate all other types of reading:

> One must deal cleanly with the Scriptures. From the very beginning the word has come to us in various ways. It is not enough simply to look and see whether this is God's word, whether God has said it; rather we must look and see to whom it has been spoken, whether it fits us. That makes all the difference between night and day.[18]

For Luther the literal sense of Scripture was given priority over all symbolic or mystical readings.[19] This privileged the obvious, "literal" meaning of the text in its context.

Luther's commitment to the literal sense was based on his belief that the Scripture is "perspicuous."[20] This meant he believed that the Bible's meaning would be clear to those who were (finally!) free to read it in their own language. At this point we need to recall the significance of Luther's translation of the Bible into German, making the Bible accessible to the public in an unprecedented way. Luther's confidence in the clarity of Scripture was grounded in his theological conviction that the entire Scripture points to Christ. The message of the Bible, both Old and New Testaments, finally is a message that foretells and proclaims the coming of Jesus Christ and his gospel. Moreover, the Scripture continues to declare the gospel of Jesus Christ as its central message to readers and hearers yet today. This is most certainly clear!

In those certain passages where the meaning of the Bible is confusing or ambiguous, Luther employed the principle that the "Scripture interprets itself."[21] Because Scripture is its own highest authority (versus Rome and the enthusiasts who appealed to other authorities), one searches the rest of the Bible to shed light on any particular texts that seem obscure. Insofar as the overall meaning of Scripture is abundantly clear in its witness to Christ and the gospel, Luther trusted the Holy Spirit to enlighten the interpretation of those disputed texts which would need to be understood through the lens of those that are crystal clear. This is a principle of interpretation that deserves our attention yet today, as we wrestle with passages about which there is no agreement. How do we appeal to passages about which there is widespread consensus as we seek to navigate the significance of contested texts for the life of the church?

After the emergence of modern historical critical methods of interpretation, discernment of the literal sense of Scripture has become increasingly complicated. Sorting through the immense volume of (and often conflicting) findings by scholars is an overwhelming task. Moreover, we are confronted with Bultmann's dictum that "exegesis without presuppositions is not possible."[22] Nonetheless, in order to provide a baseline for all subsequent interpretation, it remains useful—even necessary—for us in our efforts at understanding to begin with the literal sense of Scripture as the normative starting point for all subsequent interpretation. By "literal" sense we mean the effort to understand how a given text functioned in the life of the earliest community to which it was directed.[23] This definition allows for and authorizes the use of a variety of exegetical methods which contribute to the retrieval of the literal sense of the text.

## 4. Law and Gospel (*Lex et evangelium*)

A distinctively Lutheran contribution to the ecumenical conversation about biblical interpretation involves the use of the law-gospel paradigm to understand what God says to us in Scripture. This is a particularly Lutheran theological (not exegetical!) proposal within the history of interpretation. Luther recognized God to be speaking to humanity in the Bible with two voices: Law and Gospel. These voices are to be carefully distinguished, although never separated, in the task of biblical interpretation. It is important from the outset to make clear that the law-gospel distinction should not be equated with the difference between the Old and New Testaments. For Luther both Law and Gospel are communicated in each testament, gospel in the Old as well as law in the New Testament. Luther wrote this about the character of the Old Testament:

> Here you will find the swaddling cloths and the manger in which Christ lies, and to which the angel points the shepherds [Luke 2:12]. Simple and lowly are these swaddling cloths, but dear is the treasure, Christ, who lies in them.[24]

While the New Testament has the gospel as its most authentic content, Law and Gospel are communicated in both testaments.

When we interpret the Scripture as Law and Gospel, we turn our attention away from the literal text of the Bible and focus instead on the message being communicated. When the Word functions as law, it strikes the hearer as "demand," the demand to think in a certain way or to perform certain actions in order to fulfill either human expectations or divine righteousness. The Word of God as law leaves the hearer to rely on his/her own resources in satisfying whatever is required. According to the "first use" of the law, the requirements have to do with what society expects of us—as members of a family, workers at our jobs, citizens of a country, and members of the church. According to the "second use" of the law, the requirements have to do with what God expects of us, the fulfillment of the divine law, particularly as summarized in the Ten Commandments. On the one hand, confronted by God's requirements for our lives according to the second use of the law, we always fall short of fulfilling God's demands. On the other hand, while the human being has some capacity to fulfill society's expectations according to the first use of the law, we also fall short in this category in completing all that is expected of us. This situation led Luther to the conclusion that "the law always accuses."[25] By our own effort and works, we always fail to satisfy the letter of the law. Accordingly, the spiritual function of the law is to convince us of our sinfulness and prepare us to receive the gospel of Jesus Christ.

If the law places our lives under a demand, the character of the gospel is to extend God's unconditional promise.[26] In Jesus Christ God speaks a Word of irrevocable grace, pardon, and hope: "Christ died for you!" "Your sins are forgiven!" "For Christ's sake you will inherit eternal life!" The Scripture is replete with texts that communicate this good news. For Luther, the ultimate purpose of the Bible is only fulfilled when it serves as the vehicle for the proclamation of the gospel. This means that the Bible itself is the Word of God only in an instrumental sense. Above all, the Word of God refers to Jesus Christ himself and to the living presence of Christ in the proclaimed gospel.[27] The Bible serves as a means of grace for bringing this Word of God to us, the gospel of Jesus Christ. Luther's view of Law and Gospel is well described by Prenter:

> Luther's view of Scripture can therefore be summarized thus: the Word as letter is law. As the letter it simply places us before a history which can only call us to be imitators. As the letter it places us alone on our own resources. As preaching, however, the Word is gospel. In the form of preaching the Word is a promise of the coming of the Spirit of God and his work in us.[28]

The Bible serves as a means for the living proclamation of the Word. It is the Holy Spirit that finally determines how the hearer of the Word receives the biblical message, whether as law or as gospel. The same message might be heard by one person as law, while the same message is received as gospel by another.

Lutheran interpretation of the Bible in our time must continue to appropriate this foundational insight from Luther about Law and Gospel. The task of interpretation is not accomplished merely by undertaking scholarly exegesis, as indispensable as that may be. Rather, biblical scholarship must be put in service of the proclamation of God's Word by the church. Those who teach and preach the Bible in the Lutheran tradition must be attuned to the performance of Scripture as Law and Gospel.

Finally, for Luther, only when the Bible is proclaimed as Law and Gospel does it become the living Word of God again in our midst.

## 5. Christ the center (*Was Christum treibet*)

"In the beginning was the Word, and the Word was with God, and the Word was God. He was in the beginning with God. All things came into being through him, and without him not one thing came into being. What has come into being in him was life, and the life was the light of all people" (John 1:1-4). As Luther sailed the ocean of God's Word, the North Star which served as his compass was Jesus Christ. Jesus Christ is the Word of God in its primary meaning. The witness of Scripture is finally to serve the proclamation of the crucified and risen Jesus Christ. As we continue to interpret the Bible for our lives today, Luther would have us acknowledge that Christ is the center of Scripture, who gives significance to the whole.

In his "Theses Concerning Faith and Law" (1535), Luther even went so far as to declare that biblical texts must either refer to Christ or "must not be held to be true Scriptures." He consistently used the criterion of *was Christum treibet* (whatever preaches Christ) to determine the relative status of the biblical texts.[29]

Luther, accordingly, employed the centrality of the message about Christ as a criterion for measuring the relative value of the different voices within Scripture itself. On the basis of their witness to Christ, thereby, Luther deemed the books of James and Revelation to be of lesser importance and perhaps not worthy of inclusion in the New Testament at all![30]

One way of distinguishing among different ecumenical traditions within the whole of Christianity is by attending to their interpretation of Scripture. Varied Christian churches find the warrant for their chief convictions from different voices within the Bible: Roman Catholics emphasize the role of St. Peter as the primate to whom was entrusted authority in the church, Reformed traditions stress divine sovereignty in election and the Christian life lived to the glory of God, Methodists accent the sanctified life lived in response to God's grace, and Pentecostals focus on the gifts of the Holy Spirit manifest in the life of believers and the Christian community. The Lutheran tradition, by contrast, has placed primary focus on those biblical passages that testify to the justification of sinners by God's grace through faith in Jesus Christ alone: *Solus Christus!*

While the Bible is authoritative in each denomination, where one places the main accent within the whole counsel of Scripture becomes the basis for denominational distinctiveness. In significant ways, the differences between Christian denominations can be understood as contrasting claims about what is at the center of the Bible's message.[31]

The Lutheran movement can be considered a proposal to the whole Christian church about what should be considered the center of Scripture: the doctrine of justification by grace through faith in Jesus Christ alone.[32] The centrality of the gospel of Jesus Christ in the Bible is sometimes referred to as the Lutheran "canon within the canon." This means that in the interpretation of Scripture, the Lutheran confessions instruct us to give priority to the message of the gospel. While matters of the law (first or second use) have great significance for life in the world, these matters always remain penultimate in significance (Bonhoeffer).[33] The ultimate truth of Scripture is that we are justified by grace through faith in Jesus Christ alone. Lutherans claim "Christ alone" as the Bible's central teaching. Texts that function as prescriptions of the law are to be taken with great seriousness by the church. But finally, texts of legal significance are relative to the message about the justifying grace of God in Jesus Christ. This is not antinomianism. It is properly distinguishing Law and Gospel.[34] The penultimate law always is heard in relationship to the ultimate message of the gospel, God's justifying grace in Jesus Christ.

## 6. The proper use of reason (*Vernunft*)

"Reason is the devil's greatest whore."[35] This is likely the most famous quote of Luther on the significance of reason. Richard Dawkins and other great despisers of religion have made much use of this sentiment to discredit religious belief.[36] However, taking this quote out of context seriously distorts Luther's understanding of human reason. Just as Luther distinguished between two uses of the law, so also it is necessary to distinguish between his two "uses" of reason. When Luther wrote his diatribe against Erasmus lambasting free will and reason, he was referring to their use in cooperating to achieve salvation (matters of the right hand kingdom). Against such a use of reason, Luther lifted up a shout of protest. Only Jesus Christ works salvation! Neither works, nor free will, nor reason has any place here! In the civic realm (or the left hand kingdom), by contrast, reason is one of the most excellent gifts of God to humanity, according to Luther. When considering matters of the created realm (not the realm of salvation), we are to employ reason to analyze and understand the world in the best possible way. For this reason Luther was always a staunch proponent of the value of education. The Lutheran church, following him, is one of the leaders in supporting public education and higher education.

The particular form of reasoning appropriate to the interpretation of the Bible is called hermeneutics.[37] Hermeneutics refers to the art of interpreting texts. In reflecting on the interpretive process, one extremely useful construct is the "hermeneutical circle"[38] (see figure one). In the process of biblical interpretation, the hermeneutical circle begins with the assertion that God has spoken something to somebody through the words of a particular text of Scripture. In pursuit of the literal sense of this passage, the interpreter must attend to multiple aspects: the text itself (including attention to author, possible oral traditions, redactions), the audience (including attention to social location, time, place), the occasion of writing (including attention to purpose, rhetoric), and the world of the text (including attention to cultural milieu, religious environment, history). Employing as many exegetical methods of interpretation as the peculiarities of the text warrants,

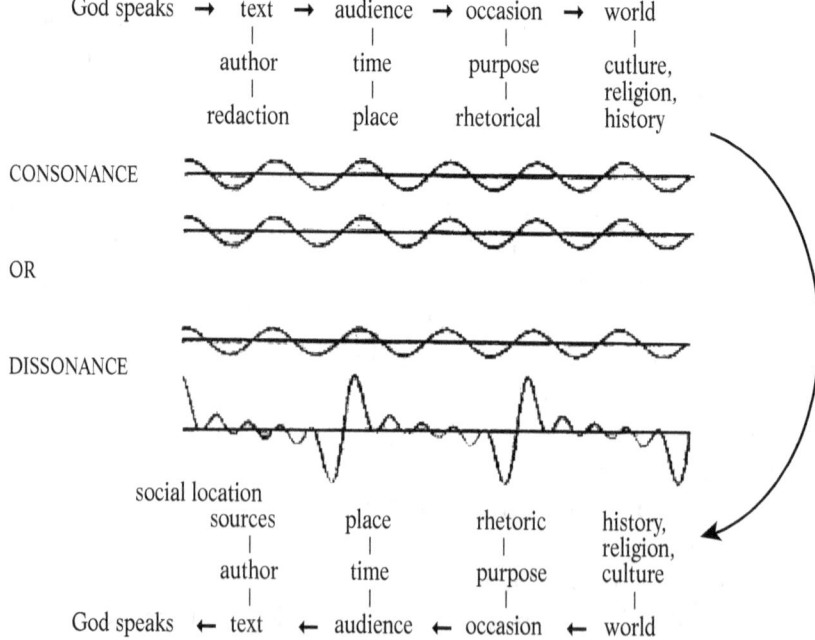

*Figure One: Hermeneutical Circle*

the interpreter arrives at some conclusions about its literal sense, that is, how the text functioned in the life of the earliest community to which it was directed. In the life of the church, these conclusions serve as the foundation for the proclamation the text, just as the literal sense serves normatively in interpreting the meaning of the text.

For Lutherans, however, interpreting the Bible does not conclude with the first half of the hermeneutical circle. Biblical texts are for proclamation![39] The completion of the circle entails close attention to the context for which the text is claimed to be authoritative: the world of the interpreter (including attention to culture, religious environment, history), the occasion (including attention to purpose, rhetoric), the audience (including attention to social location, time, place), and message (including attention to author/interpreter, sources).[40] As an outcome of interpretation, the interpreter dares to believe that God once again is speaking through the text, Law and Gospel.

How does one evaluate the legitimacy of interpretation, given the complexities of the hermeneutical process? The aim of interpretation is to create consonance between the literal sense of the text and the claims for significance to the present hearers. In a consonant performance of the text, there is recognizable congruity between its speaking to the earliest community to whom it was directed and speaking of the text to a particular community today. While the two performances are not identical, the interpreter can render account for the inevitable dissonance between the literal sense of the text and the claims about its authority in the present. In some cases, the very acknowledgment of the dissonance may serve to create a greater sense of consonance. There are occasions, however, where the contemporary performance of the biblical text may degenerate to the point where there is virtually no correspondence with its literal sense. In such instances, the dissonances are so prevalent that we can only describe the performance as failed. The hermeneutical circle has broken down, and one must begin anew with a fresh interpretation of the text.

Hermeneutical reasoning is a complex activity, analogous more to an art than a science. Such reasoning is indispensable to the process of interpretation, in spite of its fallibility. As we shall yet see, it is finally the faith community that renders verdict on the legitimacy of any particular reading of Scripture.

## 7. Living voice of the gospel (*Viva vox evangelii*)

"For as the rain and snow come down from heaven, and do not return there until they have watered the earth, making it bring forth and sprout, giving seed to the sower and bread to the eater, so shall my word be that goes out from my mouth; it shall not return to me empty, but it shall accomplish that which I purpose, and succeed in the thing for which I sent it" (Isaiah 55:10-11). The Word of God is dynamic in speaking the gospel throughout the ages. We are not the first generation to have sailed on these waters. Instead, beginning with the earliest church, every generation in every new context has heard God speaking in its own time and place. This is the Spirit's work, to bring the Bible to life so that it speaks God's Word anew in every generation.

Another fruitful concept from hermeneutical theory is the proposal that texts possess a "surplus of meaning."[41] The significance of a given text is not exhausted by how it functioned in the earliest community to which it was directed. Instead, especially for Scripture, the biblical text becomes the living voice of God in ever new contexts of interpretation where it functions once again as Word of God for new hearers. Over time, Bible texts continue to mean new things to new people in new settings.

The notion that biblical texts have a surplus of meaning entails that they invite new and fresh interpretations in ever emerging contexts. For example, consider how Augustine in the fourth century, Luther at the time of the Reformation, and preachers of every generation, including now, have interpreted the same biblical texts for their contemporaries. Dare we claim that every new interpretation adds a new layer of meaning to the text? This is indeed the destiny of biblical texts as they are interpreted over time. Every new interpreter in every new context adds another layer to the tradition of interpretation (see figure two).

As we understand God speaking through Scripture, the living voice of the gospel in ever new contexts and generations, it boggles the mind to imagine the diversity of possible interpretations and proclamations that can and have been offered for the same text. We have already contended that the literal sense of the text has normative significance for the process of interpretation. Yet, as any preacher knows, the interpretation of Scripture in sermons is no mere reiteration of the literal sense. Rather, every new rendering is carried out in its own particular hermeneutical setting (including world situation, occasion, audience, and message) that leads to the disclosure of new significance.

A flood of questions soon emerge: How does one discern whether a new interpretation is legitimate or not? Are there interpretations that are to be rejected? On what basis would one determine the difference between a legitimate and an illegitimate reading? Postmodern sensibilities are troubled by such questions. Radical reader-response criticism, for example, affirms there are an infinite number of readings, none of which should be deemed more or less legitimate.

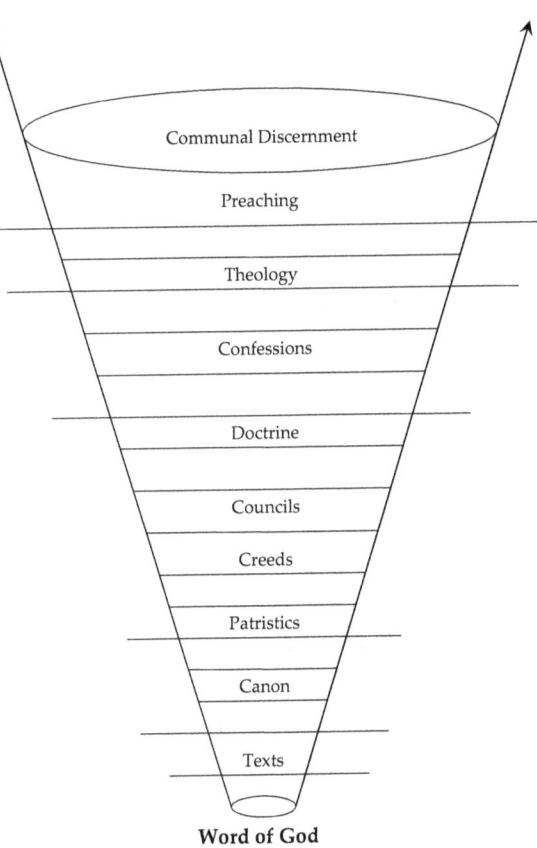

*Figure Two: The Traditioning Process*

Deconstruction becomes wary of all attempts to impose authority over the process of interpretation. The claim that there is such a thing as legitimate and illegitimate readings finds itself in acute tension with those postmodern interpreters who argue that no interpretation deserves normative significance, lest it become the basis for oppression and control.

Among the people of God, however, the interpretation of the Bible has always been understood as part of the church's traditioning process. The original speaking of the text, how it functioned in the earliest community to which it was first directed, serves as the norm for all subsequent interpretation. Later interpreters are challenged to seek consonance between the meaning of the text in its original speaking and the speaking of the text in their own context. Thereby, it might be asserted that subsequent interpretations should never say "less" than the literal sense of the text.

The literal sense should not be contradicted by later acts of interpretation. However, according to the surplus of meaning by which texts have the power to transcend their original speaking, it is possible to say "more" than it had ever previously said. Each text has a reservoir of meaning that is drawn upon in ever new acts of interpretation.

The history of interpretation, like sedimentary stone under the ocean, is composed of layer upon layer of meanings deposited over time. One of the most consequential decisions for the history of interpretation was the establishing of the biblical canon itself. As we know from the vast array of apocryphal writings, there was not always agreement about which were to be the authoritative writings. Prior to the establishment of the canon, many other texts circulated with their own claims to authority. Eventually only the canonical texts emerged with authority as God's Word and became the basis for the church's proclamation. Had other writings been deemed canonical, the traditioning process as we know it might have run a quite different course.

Once deemed canonical, each Scripture text has its own history of interpretation, vastly complex. Within this history, certain readings have become classic (for example, those by the church fathers, doctors, and reformers of the church). Classical readings are those that warrant serious engagement by later interpreters.[42] Other readings have been declared normative, especially at times of acute controversy in the history of the church (for example, the formulation of the creeds, the decisions of councils, or the forging of confessions). Such normative readings have been established by the church to regulate all subsequent interpretation.[43] Still other readings have been judged deficient, distorted, misleading, or even dangerous. These readings have been excluded by the church in the traditioning process and in some cases even declared as heresy.

Each generation is faced with the challenge of interpreting Scripture authentically in its own time and place. Interpreters are challenged to create consonance between the speaking of the text as it functioned for the earliest community to which it was directed and the present hermeneutical context. Every new interpretation is added as another layer to the traditioning process. Moreover, in every generation there emerges a contest to distinguish legitimate from illegitimate readings.[44] To discern the Word of God amid all the human words is a communal task of the church in every generation.

## 8. Discerning the Word: The contest of interpretations

One of the perennial questions facing the church in its interpretation of Scripture is how to negotiate among the competing claims within the Bible itself. Based on the same Bible, some claim it legitimate to employ violence to resolve conflict, while others only allow for nonviolent measures. From the same authoritative Scripture, some hold it necessary to be "born again" through a decision for Christ, while others hold infant baptism to be a legitimate path to salvation. From the authority of the same Word of God, some make predictions about those things that are occurring in these end times, while others hold that no one knows either the day or the hour of Christ's return. There are plenteous instances how those committed to biblical authority wrangle with one another in making competing claims about what the Bible really says.

As we have already heard, the Lutheran confessional tradition can be understood as a proposal to the whole Christian church about what should be considered the center of Scripture: the doctrine of justification by grace through faith in Jesus Christ alone (see figure three). Lutherans give priority to the gospel in the interpretation of biblical texts. As Lutherans enter the sea of contested interpretations, what they bring to the conversation (which is particular to the Lutheran confession) is insistence on Jesus Christ and the gospel as the most important matter of all.

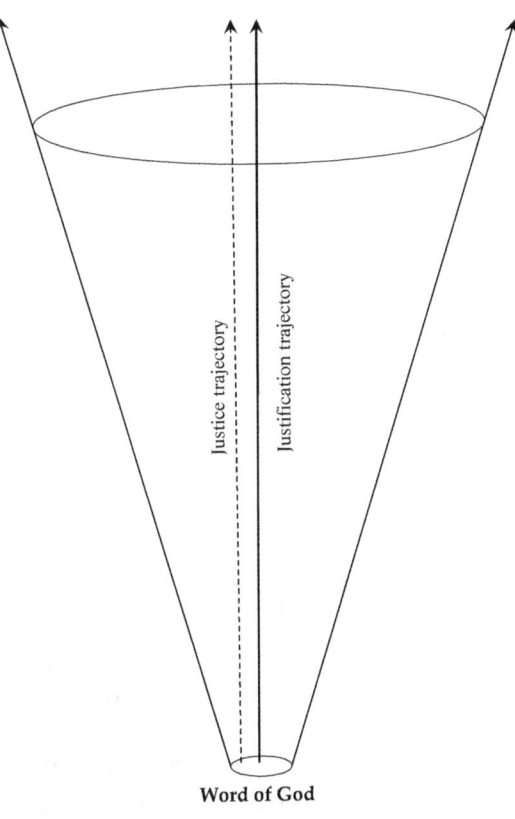

*Figure Three: Canon within the Canon*

This does not mean inattention to the literal sense of particular biblical texts. But it does mean focused theological attention on what Lutherans confess as the center of the whole counsel of Scripture, the gospel of Jesus Christ.

Other Christian traditions bring their own claims about what is most central in Scripture to this contest of interpretations. One of the most provocative proposals in recent times comes from places of extreme poverty and injustice. Out of the context of the poor in Latin America, the hungry and sick in Africa, the Dalits in India, or the African-American community in the United States, the question has been posed: Is there not at the heart of Scripture overwhelming testimony to God's concern for justice? This is nothing less than a dramatic proposal to the whole church about another canon within the canon. If Lutherans propose that the gospel with its justification trajectory is a canon within the canon of Scripture, the churches of the impoverished world ask whether there is not also a justice trajectory within Scripture that we must heed.[45] This justice trajectory begins with God hearing the cries of the slaves in Egypt, continues with the Exodus, is encoded in the laws of Israel in defense of the poor, establishes expectations for kings to do justice, and ignites in the words of the prophets. It concludes with Jesus' own concern for the dawning of God's just and peaceable kingdom expressed in his teaching, practice, cross, and resurrection. As Lutherans propose that Scripture is centered on God's saving grace in Jesus Christ, how do we respond to the proposal from the poor of this world that there is a justice trajectory which is core to the Holy Bible?

Finally, it falls to the church to deliberate which readings of Scripture are consonant with the literal sense, which are marginal readings, and even which are excluded readings (see figure four). Such a process within the church can be and usually is tempestuous. It is a process that the members of the church need to enter in a spirit of prayerfulness. Every generation engages in its own contests over the authority and meaning of Scripture. The Reformation itself was in many ways a contest over the proper interpretation of Scripture: Were Luther and the other reformers correct in their theological claim that the gospel of grace in Jesus Christ is the central message of the Bible upon which they implemented their reforms? More recent generations have battled over matters such as the legitimacy of slavery or the status of women in the life of the church, arguing over how to read Scripture on these questions. Today one intense contest rages over what the Bible has to say about homosexuality and the place of gay and lesbian persons in the church. One of the great complications in this contest involves the conflicting paradigms employed to interpret the pertinent Bible passages.[46] How does a church that affirms Scripture as the final norm for the church's faith and life negotiate conflicted interpretations of the Bible itself? This is a contemporary example of what is always at stake as the church engages in communal deliberation over the interpretation of Scripture today.

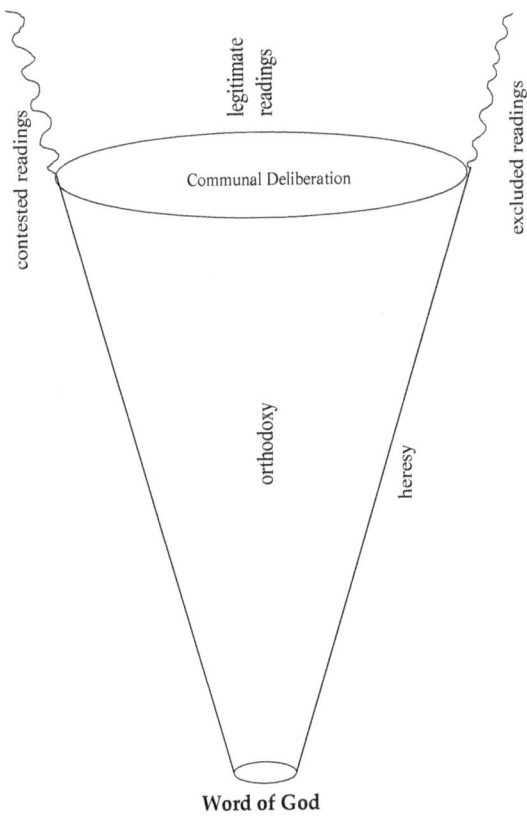

Figure Four: Communal Deliberation

We who are the church in this generation are called upon to enter the fray of contested interpretations with integrity and charity, employing our best exegetical skills and wisdom to understand the literal sense of biblical texts and to create consonance between that literal sense and the proclamation needed in our own context. We are those who are responsible for the new layers of meaning added to the tradition of interpretation in our time. We are those who are called upon to participate in the communal process of negotiating which interpretations are considered legitimate and which are precluded. We are those who are summoned to pray for the Spirit's guidance as we seek to remain faithful to God's living Word in our time.

## Conclusion

Each generation faces controversy about the proper interpretation and use of Scripture. In our time such debates are complicated both by literalist claims and postmodern sensibilities. Literalists claim that Scripture must be interpreted so that each verse supports their established theological framework.[47] In this system, the Bible serves as the basis for fixed doctrinal assertions about God and the world. Metaphor becomes proof. The central purpose of the Bible is to give us the truths (propositional revelation) we need to understand God correctly and live our lives obediently. Because of the prominence of this type of biblical interpretation in the media, many people—including many Lutherans—have been influenced by this approach. This creates a major challenge for teachers and pastors of the Lutheran church: to present a credible alternative to literalist and fundamentalist interpretation. How do we begin to undertake the immense challenge of teaching and preaching the Bible with integrity, given the influence of literalist approaches?

A completely different but also challenging undertaking involves our engagement with postmodern approaches, many of which grant the Bible no special status or particular authority. In this postmodern climate there is a major tendency to resist all normative readings of the Bible as Scripture. Instead, every individual person claims authority to read the Bible idiosyncratically: "This is what it means to me." In the postmodern context, the Bible has many meanings, depending on my own perspective or that of my subculture. All these readings exist side by side with none daring to claim anything approaching universal validity. While this postmodern situation promotes the virtue of tolerance toward difference, it undermines any and all claims to the "truth" of Scripture for the life and mission of the church. If in the case of literalism, the meaning of Scripture is zealously over-determined, in many postmodern readings it is woefully under-determined.

A Lutheran approach to the interpretation of Scripture for our time must navigate a course between the tsunami of literalism and the undertow of postmodernity. In this essay I have charted eight instructions, grounded in the Lutheran theological tradition, for a distinctive mode of biblical interpretation: God speaks, finite human words bear the infinite Word of God, the privileging of the literal sense, attending to how Scripture functions as Law and Gospel, Christ as the center of the biblical message, the proper use of hermeneutical reasoning, honoring the living voice of God in the traditioning process, and the church's task of discerning God's Word in the messy business of conflicting readings. It is my intention that these reflections help elucidate what the ELCA constitution carefully states about the nature of Scripture:

> The canonical Scriptures of the Old and New Testaments are the written Word of God. Inspired by God's Spirit speaking through their authors, they record and announce God's revelation centering in Jesus Christ. Through them God's Spirit speaks to us to create and sustain Christian faith and fellowship for service in the world.[48]

May these Lutheran insights into the interpretation of Scripture assist in guiding the church as it sails toward harbor through tempestuous waters, confident of God's providence as God speaks the Word we need to hear for the voyage in our time!

## Endnotes

1. The occasion giving rise to the subtile of this chapter was the location of my Hein-Fry lectures: once on the Gulf of Mexico and twice near the Pacific Ocean.
2. Among the ELCA's resources is Diane Jacobson, Stanley N. Olson, and Mark Allan Powell, O*pening the Book of Faith: Lutheran Insights for Bible Study* (Minneapolis: Augsburg Fortress, 2008).
3. More accurately defined as "rip currents."
4. Cf. Robin Parry, "Reader-Response Criticism," in Kevin J. Vanhoozer, ed., *Dictionary for Theological Interpretation of the Bible* (Grand Rapids: Baker Academic, 2005), 658-661.
5. Cf. A.K.M. Adam, *What Is Postmodern Biblical Criticism?* (Minneapolis: Fortress Press, 1995), 27-30.
6. Note the important distinction between "literalism" which is used to refer to verbal inspiration and propositional revelation as represented in fundamentalism and "literal sense" which describes Luther's approach to Scripture.
7. See James Barr, *The Scope and Authority of the Bible* (Philadelphia: Westminster, 1980), 65-90.
8. Cf. Craig L. Nessan, "The Authority of Scripture," *The Lutheran* online, <http://www.thelutheran.org/doc/extras/nessan.pdf>
9. Yves M. J. Congar, *I Believe in the Holy Spirit*, Vol. 3, trans. David Smith (New York: Seabury, 1983), 271.
10. Regin Prenter, *Spiritus Creator: Luther's Concept of the Holy Spirit*, trans. John M. Jensen (Philadelphia: Muhlenberg Press, 1953), 102.

11. *Ibid.*
12. *Ibid.*, 129-130.
13. Paul Althaus, *The Theology of Martin Luther*, trans. Robert C. Schultz (Philadelphia: Fortress Press, 1966), 391-399.
14. George Wolfgang Forell, "Why Recall Luther Today," *Word and World* 3/4(1983): 341.
15. Willem Jan Kooiman, *Luther and the Bible*, trans. John Schmidt (Philadelphia: Muhlenberg Press, 1961), 227-228.
16. *Ibid.*, 237.
17. Martin Luther, *Luthers Werke*, Weimar Ausgabe 16: 82, as quoted in *ibid.*, 237-238.
18. Martin Luther, "How Christians Should Regard Moses," in *Luther's Works* 35:170.
19. Bernard Lohse, *Martin Luther's Theology: Its Historical and Systematic Development*, trans. Roy A. Harrisville (Minneapolis: Fortress Press, 1999), 190.
20. Cf. Robert W. Jenson, "Luther's Contemporary Theological Significance," in Donald K. McKim, ed., *The Cambridge Companion to Martin Luther* (Cambridge: Cambridge University Press, 2003), 284-286.
21. Althaus, *The Theology of Martin Luther*, 76-78.
22. Cf. Rudolf Bultmann, "Is Exegesis without Presuppositions Possible?" in *Existence and Faith*, intro. and trans. Schubert M. Ogden (New York: Meridian, 1960), 289-296.
23. Cf. Mark Allan Powell, "How Can Lutheran Insights Open Up the Bible?" in Jacobson, et. al., *Opening the Book of Faith*, 37, who describes the "plain sense" to mean "passages are to be understood in the sense that would have seemed obvious to their original readers."
24. Martin Luther, "Preface to the Old Testament," in *Luther's Works* 35:236.
25. Werner Elert, *Law and Gospel*, trans. Edward H. Schroeder (Philadelphia: Fortress Press, 1967), 7-13.
26. Oswald Bayer, "Luther as an Interpreter of Holy Scripture," in McKim, *The Cambridge Companion to Martin Luther*, 75-77.
27. Ritva H. Williams, *The Bible's Importance for the Church Today* (Minneapolis: Augsburg Fortress Publishers, 2009), 49.
28. Prenter, *Spiritus Creator*, 115.
29. Williams, *The Bible's Importance for the Church Today*, 50.
30. Regarding Luther's deliberation of the value of these books, see Kooiman, *Luther and the Bible*, 110-116.
31. In the history of the contemporary ecumenical movement we are witnessing the growing recognition that denominational differences in the interpretation of Scripture are complementary and not contradictory.

32. Eric W. Gritsch and Robert W. Jenson, *Lutheranism: The Theological Movement and Its Confessional Writings* (Philadelphia: Fortress Press, 1976), 6.

33. Dietrich Bonhoeffer, "Ultimate and Penultimate Things," in *Ethics. Dietrich Bonhoeffer's Works*, Volume 6, trans. Reinhard Krauss, Charles C. West, and Douglas W. Stott (Minneapolis: Fortress Press, 2005), 146-170.

34. Cf. Martin Luther, "How Christians Should Regard Moses," in *Luther's Works* 35:161-174, for his criteria in interpreting the law of Moses.

35. Martin Luther, "Last Sermon in Wittenberg," Second Sunday of Epiphany, January 17, 1546, in *Luthers Werke*, Weimar Ausgabe 51:126.

36. Richard Dawkins, *The God Delusion* (New York: Houghton Mifflin Harcourt, 2006), 221.

37. Cf. Hans-Georg Gadamer, *Truth and Method* (New York: Seabury, 1975).

38. Anthony C. Thiselton, "Hermeneutical Circle, " in Vanhoozer, ed., *Dictionary for Theological Interpretation of the Bible*, 281-282.

39. Cf. Gerhard O. Forde, *Theology Is for Proclamation* (Minneapolis: Augsburg Fortress Publishers, 1990).

40. It is a hermeneutical "circle" insofar as the process of interpretation continues with ever new readings of the text for ever new contexts.

41. Paul Ricouer, *Interpretation Theory: Discourse and the Surplus of Meaning* (Fort Worth: Texas Christian University Press, 1976).

42. On the significance of the term "classic" see David Tracy, *The Analogical Imagination: Christian Theology and the Culture of Pluralism* (New York: Crossroad, 1981), 99-338.

43. Cf. George A. Lindbeck, *The Nature of Doctrine: Religion and Theology in a Postliberal Age* (Louisville: Westminster John Knox Press, 1984), 32ff.

44. Cf. Paul Ricouer, *The Conflict of Interpretations: Essays in Hermeneutics*, ed. Don Ihde (Evanston: Northwestern University Press, 1974).

45. Lutherans might well consider the justice trajectory as an exposition of the first use of the law in Lutheran categories.

46. Cf. Craig L. Nessan, *Many Members, Yet One Body: Committed Same-Gender Relationships and the Mission of the Church* (Minneapolis: Augsburg Fortress Publishers, 2004), 23-37.

47. Cf. James Barr, *Fundamentalism* (Worcester: SCM, 1981), 160-186.

48. Evangelical Lutheran Church in America, *Constitution, Bylaws, and Continuing Resolutions*, Chapter 2: Confession of Faith, 2.02c.

© *Craig L. Nessan—January 2009*

# Law and Gospel and the Interpretation of Scripture

Mark Allan Powell
*Trinity Lutheran Seminary*

Law and Gospel is probably the best known Lutheran principle for interpreting Scripture. Lutherans are always talking about Law and Gospel, sometimes in ways that people in other churches do not understand—and, sometimes, in ways that other Lutherans do not understand.[1] We don't always mean the same thing by it and, as a result, some mischievous misunderstandings have been possible or prevalent.

For example, it is common to discover that non-Lutherans think that Lutherans use the expression Law and Gospel as another way of talking about Old and New Testaments. The "law" is the Old Testament and the "gospel" is the New Testament. This is not what we mean—and it is not what we believe. There is a lot of gospel in the Old Testament and there is a lot of law in the New Testament.[2]

Second, many people—including Lutherans—seem to have gotten the idea that "law" is bad and should be avoided, while "gospel" is good and should be encouraged. I hear Lutheran pastors say, "You shouldn't preach 'law,' you should preach 'gospel.'" This is also not what we believe.[3] It would be better to say, "You shouldn't preach 'just law,' you should preach 'Law and Gospel.'" It would also be correct to say, "You shouldn't preach 'just gospel,' you should preach 'Law and Gospel.'"[4]

I admit that the gospel is often more pleasant than the law, but there should be no question of avoiding one and embracing the other. It is not "pick and choose." We need both Law and Gospel.

Those are a couple of preliminary observations—nothing new to any of you, I hope. Now, let me tell you what I want to do in this paper.

First, I want to describe my basic understanding of what we do mean by Law and Gospel and, also my understanding of what we mean when we talk about "the law" in a rather different sense. It is my contention that Lutherans use the word law in two different ways—which helps to explain why what we say is often confusing and why we sometimes get confused ourselves.

This will lead to three further points:

1. Law and Gospel is a hermeneutical principle, not an exegetical one.
2. Law and Gospel is a homiletical principle; its role in biblical studies, while highly significant, is limited.
3. Law and Gospel assumes an audience-oriented or reader-response approach to Scripture. It is a tool for discerning the effects of Scripture in modern contexts, not a method for explicating the intended meaning for an original or historical context.

What will we accomplish? Well, I hope to add some clarity and provoke some reflection. I also think that I will be able to explain why the distinctively Lutheran understanding of homiletics waned during the twentieth century. And, along the way, I think that I might accidentally resolve the age-old controversy over the "third use of the law." I didn't set out to do that; it just kind of happened. Quite a lot. Let's get started.

For my basic definition of Law and Gospel look at the left-hand column of the handout (see Appendix 1).

## Law and Gospel

Lutherans say that the Word of God speaks both Law and Gospel and that these must be properly distinguished and yet also held together for God's Word to be fulfilled:

Law = that which accuses us and judges us.

Gospel = that which comforts us and saves us.

This message of Law and Gospel is at the heart of Scripture: Faithful interpretation discerns this message; faithful proclamation declares this message.

There are many Lutheran writings that try to define what the terms Law and Gospel mean and what they include.[5] Carl Braaten, in his *Principles of Lutheran Theology*, says the law is that which "accuses, condemns, denounces, punishes, and kills"; the gospel is that which "comforts, strengthens, forgives, liberates, and renews."[6] Paul Althaus says, "The law places a man under the wrath of God; the gospel brings grace."[7]

At Trinity Lutheran Seminary, where I teach, Walter Bouman liked to speak of law as "existential dread" and gospel as "eschatological hope." Don Luck would describe law as "that which reveals our human brokenness" and gospel as "that which heals our human brokenness." Cheryl Peterson, our current systematic theologian, says, "The law convicts us; the gospel delivers us." Tim Huffman adds that the law promotes anxiety, feeding our suspicion that we are insignificant and unworthy; the gospel assures us of our importance to God and of our place in God's world—we are not trivial; we have a mission, to serve God and neighbor.[8]

I think we can agree that these are different ways of talking about the same reality. And while people may clearly prefer one set of terms to another, all of these descriptions seem to cohere with what I have put in shorthand on the handout: The law accuses and judges; the gospel comforts and saves.

But, now, to shift gears somewhat, let us note that Lutherans also talk about the two-fold use of the law—or sometimes, the three-fold use of the law. This is in the right-hand column of the hand-out.

What is the function or use of "the law"? Notice we are not, at this point, talking about the function or use of the gospel. Just "the law." What is the function or use of the law?

First, the law serves the political function of maintaining a semblance of order in society.[9] People are not able to keep the law in a way that satisfies God's righteousness: They cannot be justified or put right with God by the law, but people can keep the law to an extent that allows for a certain civic righteousness. This is significant because otherwise the world would be in such total chaos that it would be impossible for the church to exist as an institution or to exercise its mission.[10]

Second, the law serves the theological function of showing us our need for the gospel.[11] This is clearly what interests Luther the most, for this is the role that the law plays in justification.[12] By revealing the holy will of God, the law exposes human sin. Confronted with such a reality, according to Luther, we are horrified and brought to despair . . . that is, we are brought to despair of anything save trust in Christ alone.[13]

And, finally, Lutherans sometimes say that the law may also serve the ethical or catechetical function of teaching us right from wrong.

There is a famous controversy in Lutheranism over this "third use." The initial problem is that Martin Luther himself does not mention it when he writes about the uses or functions of the law, though Melanchthon does,[14] and the three-fold use also appears in the Formula of Concord (Article VI). Obviously Luther believed that the Bible sometimes teaches people right from wrong, but he does not say that this is the function of the law. So, many Lutherans have wanted to insist that the law has only two uses—political and religious. Others insist on the three uses, claiming that for Luther the ethical or catechetical function was implied or simply assumed.

Here is my analysis of that argument. I think that the word law is used to mean two rather different things. The law that Lutherans refer to when they talk about Law and Gospel is not the same thing as the law that Lutherans talk about when they discuss the various uses or functions of the law. Martin Luther himself was not absolutely consistent on this, though most of the time when he talks about Law and Gospel he seems to mean something different from what the Formula of Concord means when it says that the law has three uses.

On the handout I give two different definitions of the word law. These are my definitions, not Luther's.

First, with regard to Column A, when we are talking about law in the sense of Law and Gospel, we are referring to God's standard of righteousness. We are referring to the holy will of God in light of which all human endeavors are judged.[15] Biblical commandments (that is, laws) may exemplify this or testify to it, but according to both Luther and Paul, the law in the sense of God's holy standard of righteousness is written on human hearts.[16] We are talking about a generic and yet absolutely fundamental sense of good and evil.[17]

If this is what we mean by law, what is its function?[18] When sinful humanity is confronted with the holy will of God, the response is twofold:

first, feeble efforts at compliance. While these are doomed to failure and absolutely worthless in terms of justification, they do produce a basic semblance of order that allows for society to function without total chaos. And second—and by far most important—the law, when defined as God's standard of righteousness, drives us to despair and shows us our need of the gospel. It is a word that judges and accuses.

Does it have a "third use"? I think not. God's standard of righteousness—holiness, if you will—does not serve to teach us right from wrong. What Luther has in mind when he speaks of the law in Law and Gospel is something much more profound than legal dos and don'ts. What Luther perceives is that the divine will is consummate with God's holy nature, such that what the law requires is not mere obedience to this or that regulation, but absolute holy perfection, equal to that of God. Nothing else can stand in God's sight. Nothing else satisfies. Nothing else is acceptable. Nothing else even qualifies for consideration. But if this is what the law is—a revelation of God's holiness—then I do not see how it could teach us anything that our minds could possibly comprehend. When we gaze in awe upon God's holiness, we do not take notes regarding this or that aspect of God's holy character that we might, with a bit more effort, be able to emulate. No, we tremble at the horrifying realization that we are not simply ignorant or ineffective or lackadaisical or unmotivated. We are sinners. We are the opposite of holy, and nothing we say, think, or do can change that.[19]

Thus, when a Lutheran pastor offers a didactic sermon that is intended to teach people the difference between right and wrong, I do not think that pastor is preaching "law" in the sense of Law and Gospel. Pastors sometimes think that this is what they are doing because they have heard about the three uses of the law, and they say, "I am preaching the third use of the law this morning." This is a mischievous misunderstanding. Preaching the law in the sense of Law and Gospel means proclaiming the holy, righteousness of God as the standard by which all human merit is to be judged. It is a word that accuses us and condemns us, not a word that catechizes us with regard to proper Christian behavior.[20]

But, then—back to my handout—the word law can also be used in another sense.

Law often refers to a genre of biblical literature, including especially commandments and other materials that relate how God wants people to live. I think that the law in this sense—biblical commandments—does obviously function to instruct people ethically, to teach them right from wrong.[21] In fact, that is the primary use and probably the only intended use. I do not think that biblical commandments function explicitly or intentionally to bring people to despair or to show them their need of the gospel. Commandments may sometimes have that effect, but it is not their intended purpose.

So, I am saying that when the "law" is understood to mean biblical commandments, then, yes, it certainly does serve in the way that the Formula of Concord calls its "third use"—namely, to teach people right from wrong. But I am also saying that this should not be called the "third" use because that implies that commandments have first and second uses to which moral instruction is subordinated. Commandments (or "laws," if you will) are essentially "announcements of the divine will" with regard to specific, particular, and often mundane matters. Many, perhaps most, can be obeyed —at least in the sense in which the biblical authors expected or intended them to be obeyed. I don't like referring to "moral instruction" as the third use to which commandments might sometimes be put, when it is in fact the primary use and probably the only use to which they were intended to be put.

There is, of course, some sense in which biblical commandments point to the holy righteousness of God and, obviously, any revelation of God's righteousness will bring people to despair and show them their need of the gospel. But that is a function of God's standard of righteousness, not a function of the commandments as such. The commandments themselves were given to teach people how God wants them to live, and that should be recognized as their primary and most important function.

In the Small Catechism, in the section on the Ten Commandments, Luther asks repeatedly, "What does this [commandment] mean?" And each time, he says that the meaning of the commandment is that God wants us to do something or not do something. Never once does he say that the meaning of the commandment is that we are to be driven to despair and realize our need for the gospel.

In short, I believe there is a difference between the law and "laws." The distinction between the two is analogous to the difference between sin and "sins." Laws try to deal with the problem of sins. As Lutherans we are often quick to say that "laws" (or commandments) do not deal very effectively with sins because we are unable to keep these commandments or to obey these laws. That may often be true, but it is a limited, reductionist understanding of the problem. Even if we were able to keep all of the commandments —all of the "laws"—we would still be sinners. And this is what the law reveals; this is what the law that we refer to in Law and Gospel does; it reveals that we are sinners, quite apart from the fact that we fail to obey individual laws and often commit particular sins. We are not sinners because we sin; rather, we sin because we are in fact sinners. And the law does not accuse us because it consists of laws; rather, "laws" accuse us because they witness to the law (they bear witness to the holiness of God in light of which all human merit is to be judged).

We began by saying, when Lutherans talk about Law and Gospel, they do not mean Old and New Testament. Now I am saying that when Lutherans talk about Law and Gospel, they do not mean "commands and promises"—or, at least, they should not mean this. I am aware that it is very, very common in Lutheranism to hear the claim that law means commandments and gospel means promises. Many famous Lutheran theologians say this, and so do the confessions. I am not saying that it is wrong; I am saying it is limited. It is certainly a reductionist understanding of what the Apostle Paul meant by "law" and "gospel," and I suspect that it is a reductionist understanding of what Luther meant by "law" and "gospel." If we want to speak about commands and promises, we should call them that ("commands and promises"), and we should let Law and Gospel mean something greater, something more, something like "the revelation of God's true nature, the revelation of divine holiness and mercy."

Now, if this is correct, then I think that the scheme of a three-fold use of the law mixes apples with oranges: it tries to talk about the law and "laws" as though the two are synonymous.[22] The Formula of Concord basically took Luther's two uses of the law (which its authors apparently thought meant "commandments") and added a third use, one that is better attributable to "laws" than to the law proper. I have suggested a different formulation on the handout. When the word law is used to mean "God's standard of righteousness, the holy will of God," then the law functions to create basic order in society and to show us our need of the gospel. But when our English word "law" is used to mean "laws"; i.e., "biblical commandments," the clear and primary function of those laws is to tell people how God wants them to live, to teach people right from wrong. There are, then two uses of the law and one use of "laws," but not three uses unless you combine two things that probably ought to be kept separate.

Now we are about halfway done and, if you have followed me thus far, you will have already grasped what is probably the best insight that I have to offer. You might be forgiven, however, for thinking this is all a bit pedantic. The practical relevance, I believe, comes into play when we consider how the Lutheran principle of Law and Gospel is used (and misused) in biblical interpretation. I will try to clarify this with a series of three points that, I hope, will not only describe the problem but also point toward a resolution.

First, I propose that Law and Gospel is a hermeneutical principle, not an exegetical one.

I realize that the distinction between hermeneutics and exegesis can be somewhat artificial because the categories do overlap, but for our present purposes let us regard exegesis as the task of interpreting Scripture and hermeneutics as dealing with the broader question of what is meant by being "faithful to Scripture" once it has been interpreted. Hermeneutics usually assumes exegesis: Exegesis asks, "What does the Bible mean?" Hermeneutics says, "Okay, we think we know what it means. Now what?"

The Lutheran principle of Law and Gospel functions best when we are talking about this hermeneutical appropriation of Scripture. Truth be told, it does not work very well when we are trying to discern the exegetical meaning of Scripture. The usual task of exegesis is to consider texts within their historical and literary contexts and to determine the meaning that texts were originally intended to have: What did the author mean to say to the anticipated readership? It would be a mistake to assume that all biblical texts were intended by their authors as either "words that accuse and condemn" or as "words that comfort and save." Some texts are merely informative; they relay information about practices, people, places, and things. Some texts were intended to serve as aids in worship. And, as indicated already, some were intended to provide moral instruction—or just good practical advice. The problem is that overzealous Lutherans have sometimes sought to impose their principle of Law and Gospel on biblical texts in ways that ignore basic exegesis. Thus, Protestant scholasticism maintained that the primary function of Torah was to bring people to despair so that they would trust exclusively in God's grace. The role of Torah, then, was always preparatory and it was always bad news, albeit bad news intended to serve a good purpose. This makes one wonder why the psalmist would say that the law of the Lord is perfect, delighting the soul. Sweeter than honey. More to be desired than gold. Perhaps if he had been a Lutheran, he would have known better. If the psalmist had employed the Lutheran concept of Law and Gospel as an exegetical principle, he would have decided that there is nothing sweet or precious or perfect about Torah—except that it prepares one for the gospel.

But that would be bad exegesis. The exegetical meaning of Torah is not that it prepares people for the gospel. To claim that this is its purpose is to renounce any interest in authorial intent. Moses clearly did not offer Torah in order to prepare people for the gospel. The Lutheran principle is insightful at a hermeneutical level, but it must not be applied too soon, in a way that negates exegesis and prevents us from understanding the intended meaning of the text.

I'll make the same point again with a New Testament example; this one has a rich history in the annals of misinterpretation. The Sermon on the Mount is probably the best-known example of Torah in the New Testament, and for centuries the Lutheran principle of Law and Gospel led Lutheran interpreters to mis-read the text in a manner contrary to its obvious meaning. To this day, I rarely lead a program on the Sermon on the Mount among Lutheran clergy at which at least one pastor does not suggest, "Wasn't the reason Jesus told this sermon to make people realize they will never be able to live up to God's demands, and so would just have to trust in justification by faith?"

The short answer: "No." That is not why Jesus preached this sermon, and it is not why Matthew put this sermon into his gospel. This was, however, the understanding of Lutheran scholasticism, which ignored anything remotely similar to what we today would call exegesis. According to this view, the demands of the Sermon are not only harsh, they are impossible to keep.[23] And, of course, Jesus knew his demands would be impossible to keep, so it was just a trick, a big set-up. Basically, Jesus knew that someone would put his sermon in the gospel of Matthew, which would be the first book in the New Testament, followed a few books later by Romans—so Jesus set things up in a very clever fashion, articulating

God's will in a manner that would bring people to despair, knowing that if they only kept reading they would be rescued, in time, by Paul.[24]

In one of the most important works on the Sermon on the Mount ever written, Joachim Jeremias dubbed this approach "the Lutheran error."[25] Jeremias was a Lutheran himself so the error is not inevitable. Indeed, Martin Luther's own reflections on the Sermon on the Mount are wonderfully free of this "Lutheran error."

So, the Lutheran concept of Law and Gospel ought not be employed as an exegetical principle for discerning the essential meaning of texts. It may, however, be employed as a hermeneutical principle for explicating the ultimate effect of texts. The Apostle Paul provides us with a good example of how this might be done. In Romans 7, Paul says that the effect of the law is to magnify our sins in such a way that we are confronted with them. The law thus becomes the means through which sin deceives and kills, bringing death (Romans 7:7ff.). But when Paul says this, he is not writing as an exegete, claiming that he has discerned the historical intentions of Moses or of the Deuteronomic historian. He is simply describing the effect that God's Word has on sinful humanity.

Likewise, we Lutherans may recognize correctly that Law and Gospel summarizes the effects of Scripture without assuming that those effects were explicitly intended in every instance by every author. The main point is that Scripture as a whole conveys a message that accuses and condemns us, and also a message that comforts and saves us. With regard to the Sermon on the Mount, it is not exegetically sound to say that Jesus preached this Sermon in order to bring people to despair and show them their need of the gospel. Rather, he preached the sermon in order to tell people how God wanted them to live. But it may be hermeneutically sound to say that despair is an inevitable consequence of receiving this text as the words of a holy God spoken to sinful humanity.

My next point is that for Lutherans, Law and Gospel is mainly a homiletical principle. Its role in biblical studies, while highly significant, is limited.

In our ELCA constitution, we speak of God's Word in a three-fold sense: the Incarnate Word (Jesus Christ himself), the Proclaimed Word (the message of Law and Gospel), and the Written Word (the Bible). Law and Gospel applies mainly and most importantly to the proclaimed word—that is, to preaching.

In Lutheran homiletical tradition, the goal of preaching is to proclaim both Law and Gospel in the sense that we have discussed: the goal of preaching is to announce God's word that judges and condemns us and also to announce God's word that saves us and comforts us.[26]

The goal of a sermon is not to provide people with doctrinal or moral instruction; preaching is different from teaching in Lutheran tradition.[27]

Thus, when a Lutheran pastor looks at a text for Sunday morning—whether it's from the Old Testament or from the epistles or from one of the gospels—there may be all kinds of things that this text has to say. We might be able to learn some interesting things about agricultural practices in ancient Israel. Or, maybe the text tells us a story about some important person who lived a long time ago. There's nothing wrong with learning about those things—and Sunday school classes or Bible study groups may offer occasions for doing so. But when the goal is preaching, Lutheran pastors are trained to look at texts and ask two questions: Law? Gospel? What does this text say that accuses us? What does it say that comforts us? What is God's word of judgment, and what is God's word of salvation?

This hermeneutic obviously affects the way we interpret Scripture, or, I should say, it affects the way we interpret Scripture for the task of preaching. That is a significant qualifier because there are valid interpretations of Scripture that do not lead to preaching (including interpretation that supports doctrinal and moral instruction). I would not want the hermeneutic of Law and Gospel to be used in a comprehensive way for distinguishing valid interpretations of Scripture from invalid ones.

This may seem obvious but, again, let us consider how it plays out in practice. Every now and then, I hear some Lutheran maintain that, since someone else's interpretation of Scripture does not cohere with Law and Gospel, it must be a misunderstanding, a misinterpretation, an invalid use of scripture. "Lutherans are always supposed to interpret Scripture in light of Law and Gospel," this person will say. No. That is not what we believe. We say that preachers are always supposed to proclaim Scripture in light of Law and Gospel, but this is a homiletical principle that should not be used to evaluate all interpretations of Scripture, including those offered for purposes other than preaching.

I have indicated that Lutherans typically make a distinction between preaching and teaching. I want to say a bit more about this because in recent years, the distinction has eroded to the detriment of both phenomena.

In the latter half of the twentieth century, the specifically Lutheran understanding of homiletics waned.[28] I think this was a result of two things: ecumenical movements and the rise of the historical critical method for interpreting Scripture. Both were good things, but in this case they produced what I consider to be an unfortunate result.

First, let us consider the impact of ecumenical awareness. We are more in tune now with what happens in other denominations, and such awareness can produce a subtle pressure toward conformity. Many Lutherans today—preachers and congregants—don't want Lutheran sermons to sound different from sermons in other churches. Historically, our approach to preaching has been somewhat unique: The idea of the sermon as a means of grace—a liturgical act that imparts Law and Gospel to people—is quite different from the idea of the sermon as a mini-lecture or "message" (as many church bulletins now call it). But in the latter half of the twentieth century, improved relations with other churches would affect our pulpits. The preacher down the road was advertising "Three Ways to Improve Your Marriage," and Law and Gospel has a hard time competing with that, especially when that church down the road gets a new topic every week and Lutherans do not. Last Sunday, the Lutheran preacher announces, the topic of my sermon was "Law and Gospel." This week, it's "Law and Gospel." Next Sunday, it will be "Law and Gospel." Same topic every week, because for Lutherans the sermon is not viewed as part of the church's educational ministry. It is viewed as part of the church's liturgy. A sermon is a liturgical act that serves as a means of grace, imparting Law and Gospel to people.

I said that there were two things that caused this understanding to erode: first, ecumenical awareness. And, now, second, the rise of the historical critical method led to training clergy in disciplines of exegesis. But on its own, exegesis tends to translate into didactic sermons. As I have already indicated, exegesis tries to uncover the meaning of a text intended by its author, which is not always going to be what Lutherans call Law and Gospel. For preaching in the Lutheran tradition, an additional hermeneutical step is required, but seminaries have not done a stellar job of training people in how to take that step, and many pastors do not seem to have figured out how to take it on their own. What often happens is that the Lutheran preachers—just like other preachers— present the exegetically determined meaning of the text as the sermon. My claim is that exposition of the exegetically determined meaning of the text may make for a fascinating Bible study for inspirational and provocative teaching, but it does not necessarily make for proclamation of Law and Gospel.

When I go to church on Sunday morning, I want the sermon to do two things to me: I want it to make me fear God. That's the law. And I want it to make me love God. That's the gospel.

Martin Luther says in his Small Catechism, "we are to fear and love God so that . . . ," then lots of things follow. Lutheran churches should have entire forums and Bible studies and Sunday school classes devoted to the "so thats" of the catechism—and they do! But the sermon in a Lutheran church should not be a summary of "so thats."

I hear lots of didactic "so that" sermons, and I realize the preacher is trying to help me to be faithful to God. I appreciate that, but it's not what I need from a sermon. I need the Word of God to operate as a means of grace, producing in me the fear of God and the love of God.

Sometimes I think that the pastor assumes that since I feared God and loved God last week, I probably still do. We can go on with the "so thats." But I may be a worse sinner than you think.

Preach the law so that I will fear God; preach the gospel so that I will love God. Same topic every week.

My final point is that Law and Gospel assumes an audience-oriented or reader response approach to Scripture. It defines the meaning of Scripture in terms of its effect on those who receive it.

Historical critical approaches to Scripture assume an author-oriented hermeneutic. The meaning of any text is to be equated with the sense intended by its original author. Reader-response criticism, by contrast, seeks to discern the plurality of meaning that a text might generate for a variety of different readers who receive it in diverse contexts. There should be discernible trajectories between authorial intent and these diverse responses, but reader-response criticism does recognize that texts come to mean things that their authors did not specifically anticipate.

As an official approach to biblical studies, reader-response criticism is only a few decades old, but Martin Luther appears to have been 500 years ahead of his time. His hermeneutical, homiletical principle of Law and Gospel seems to assume an approach to exegetical interpretation that allows for a more dynamic concept of meaning than one that defines legitimate interpretation narrowly as expressions of explicit authorial intent. Reader-response criticism offers such an approach. The reader-response critic attempts to recognize a range of possible meanings that a text might have in various contexts, and effects congruent with what Lutherans call Law and Gospel would typically be included within this range of possible meanings.[29]

Let me try to put this another way. Traditional, historical-critical exegesis focuses on discerning the intended message of a text, while reader-response criticism focuses on elucidating anticipated effects of a text. Historical-criticism has proved useful in a great many ways, but it has not proved especially useful for interpreting Scripture for preaching, especially when preaching is construed in the Lutheran sense of proclaiming Law and Gospel. The reason, as we have seen, is that the intended message of the text might not have been to present a word that judges or a word that saves. But the goal of reader-response criticism is to elucidate anticipated effects of a text, which usually will include meanings that fit with the Lutheran principle of Law and Gospel.

Why? Because Law and Gospel are categories defined by effect, not by message or genre or content. This takes us back to the beginning.

It is a misunderstanding of Law and Gospel to equate "commands" with law and "promises" with gospel.[30] Luther thought that any text could convey either law or gospel depending on the disposition of the audience.[31]

This might become more clear with a couple of examples. Let's take the first of the Ten Commandments: "You shall have no other gods." Is that law or gospel? People who want to have other gods may indeed hear a word that accuses them and judges them. But people who do not want to have other gods—who find the notion of multiple gods oppressive—might take comfort in the offer of Yahweh to be the only God one needs to worship or serve. I can imagine any number of polytheists and idolators throughout the ages who would respond to this commandment by saying, "Only one God? That's wonderful! I've spent my life trying to appease two dozen. This is good news!" Or, as we would say, gospel. A commandment is good news—Gospel!

Or take the beloved promises of the Twenty-third Psalm: The Lord will be our Shepherd . . . lead us, guide us, protect us, provide for us. Surely that text is pure gospel, isn't it? Well, to those who want to be led and guided, it is, but, there are people in this world who would prefer to just be footloose and fancy free, without anyone telling them where to go or what to do, and the recognition that they need a shepherd may come as a word of incrimination and judgment. Indeed, my guess is that most sheep, if you could interview them, would probably not choose to have shepherds. But then, they are sheep. They may not know that green pastures and still waters sometimes have to be provided, and they might not always give adequate consideration to what I like to call "the wolf factor." But our point is simply that the likening of our relationship to God as that of sheep to shepherd might be viewed as comforting and affirming to some and as insulting or confining to others. It might be received as good news, or it might be received as a challenging word of judgment.

And this is all intended to illustrate my third thesis: the hermeneutical, homiletical principle of Law and Gospel is a tool for discerning and proclaiming the effects of Scripture.[32]

At the very bottom of the handout, I offer my summary of how the exegetical, hermeneutical, homiletical process might work:

Scripture may be faithfully exegeted so as to reveal the basic intentions of its original author. From this, we may discern a plurality of possible effects that the text might have on people in various contexts—effects that would be congruent with authorial intent even if they go beyond the specifics of such intent. And from that plurality of potential effects, the Lutheran preacher should be encouraged to select two—the accusatory effect of law and the comforting effect of gospel.

## Endnotes

[1] Some confusion results from the fact that Luther does not lay out his view systematically and that he may have used the term *law* (at least) differently in some (earlier) writings than in other (later) ones. Hendrix says, "Historically, I think Luther made up a hermeneutic as he went" (28) and "I would not, therefore, say that Luther had a single hermeneutical method or principle, but a hermeneutical

vision. By that I mean: Luther had a vision of what life under the gospel should be" (28-29). See Scott Hendrix, "The Interpretation of the Bible According to Luther and the Confessions, or Did Luther Have a (Lutheran) Hermeneutic?" in David C. Ratke, ed., *Hearing the Word: Lutheran Hermeneutics–A Vision of Life Under the Gospel* (Minneapolis: Lutheran University Press, 2006), 13-31. In any case, Melanchthon and subsequent reformers definitely used the term *law* (and possibly *gospel*) differently than Luther did, which contributes to the confusion.

2   Althaus (p. 261) says that for Luther "'Law' is everything that makes us realize our sin and accuses and terrifies the conscience, regardless of whether one finds it in Christ or in Moses." See Paul Althaus, *The Theology of Martin Luther* (Philadelphia: Fortress Press, 1956). Cf. *WA* 39, I, 348, 535. Luther finds it specifically in the Lord's Prayer *(WA* 39, I, 351).

3   *WA* 39, I, 382. See Althaus, 257.

4   Nestingen says, "Separated from the Law, the Gospel gets absorbed into an ideology of tolerance in which indiscriminateness is equated with grace. Separated from the Gospel, the Law becomes an insatiable demand hammering away at the conscience until it destroys a person." See James A. Nestingen, "Distinguishing Law and Gospel: A Functional View," *Concordia Journal* 22 (January 1996), 27. On this point, see also Timothy J.Wengert, *A Formula for Parish Practice: Using the Formula of Concord in Congregations* (Grand Rapids, Michigan: Wm. B. Eerdmans Publishing Company, 2006), 87-88. Still, the fact that both gospel and law are to be preached does not necessarily mean the two are to be given "equal weight." Luther said, in effect, that he would rather be known for preaching too much gospel than for preaching too much law—and with regard to those who criticized him on this account, he responded, "Christ himself had to hear that he was a friend of publicans and sinners . . . we shall not fare any better" (*WA* 37, 394-395).

5   But as a preliminary caution, note what Meuser says: Luther "was not primarily interested in a theoretical definition of law and gospel. Rather, he was concerned to show that nothing we do can bridge the gap, restore us to God, and give us new life . . . so long as we are still in a tug-of-war or a bargaining stance with God, we are dead. Only God's promise makes us alive and our trust in God's promise makes all questions about the worth of our efforts superfluous." See Fred W. Meuser, *Luther the Preacher* (Minneapolis: Augsburg Publishing House, 1983), 22-23.

6   Braaten, 139. See Carl E. Braaten, *Principles of Lutheran Theology*, 2nd ed. (Minneapolis: Fortress Press, 2007). Luther himself said, "The true and proper function of the law is to accuse and to kill; but the function of the gospel is to make alive." *WA* 39, I, 363.

7   Althaus, 256.

8   Walther offers a somewhat more detailed listing of the effects of law and gospel. The law demands but does not enable compliance; it hurls people into despair, for it diagnoses the disease without providing any cure; and it terrifies the conscience by producing contrition and offering no comfort. The gospel creates faith, stills every voice of accusation, and transforms people by planting love in their hearts and enabling them to do good works. See C. F. W. Walther, *The Proper Distinction Between Law and Gospel* (St. Louis: Concordia Publishing House, 2004; lectures

given in 1864-1865), 16. Cf. John T. Pless, *Handling the Word of Truth: Law and Gospel in the Church Today* (St. Louis: Concordia Publishing House, 2004), 14-15.

9  Luther writes in his 1535 Galatians commentary, "Thus the first understanding and use of the Law is to restrain the wicked. For the devil reigns in the whole world and drives men to all sorts of shameful deeds. That is why God has ordained magistrates, parents, teachers, laws, shackles, and all civic ordinances, so that, if they cannot do any more, they will at least bind the hands of the devil and keep him from raging at will" (*Luther's Works* 26:309).

10  From the second Antinomian Disputation: "Political righteousness is good and worthy of praise, though it cannot stand in the sight of God." And: "Among men, temporal righteousness has its own honor and its own reward in this life, but not with God." *WA* 39, I, 441, 456-57. Cf. Bernhard Lohse, *Martin Luther's Theology: Its Historical and Systematic Development* (Minneapolis: Fortress Press, 1999), 271.

11  Again from the Galatians commentary: "The other use of the Law is the theological or spiritual one, which serves to increase transgressions. This is the primary purpose of the Law of Moses, that through it sin might grow and be multiplied, especially in the conscience. . . . And so when the Law accuses and terrifies the conscience—"You must do this or that! You have not done so! Then you are condemned to the wrath of God and to eternal death!"—then the Law is being employed in its proper use and for its proper purpose. Then the heart is crushed to the point of despair. This use and function of the Law is felt by terrified and desperate consciences. . . . Therefore the Law is a hammer that crushes rocks, a fire, a wind, and a great and mighty earthquake that overturns mountains" (*Luther's Works* 26:309-310).

12  "For Luther the distinction between law and gospel coheres most intimately with his doctrine of justification" (Lohse, 267).

13  Althaus says the despair produced by the law is for Luther "a salutary despair" because the threats, judgment, and condemnation of the law "are not the goal but the means in God's hands" (259).

14  See Lohse, 271, n. 22; 275.

15  Althaus says, "in terms of its content, the law is the eternal will of God" (252).

16  For Paul, see Romans 1:18-21. For Luther, the first Antinomian Disputation: "All by nature have a certain knowledge of the law, though it is very weak and hazy. Hence, it was and is always necessary to hand on to them that knowledge of the law so that they may recognize the magnitude of their sin, the wrath of God, etc." *WA* 39 I, 361. Luther's understanding of the law as intrinsic to the human spirit, written on human hearts, and antedating the Decalogue is discussed by Althaus, p. 251. He cites references in *WA* 39, I, 352, 374, 402, 454, 478, 539, 540; *WA* 17, II, 102.

17  Walther emphasized this as a key distinction between law and gospel: the law is inscribed in the human heart, which is why the moral requirements of most religions are essentially the same as what is found in the Bible; the gospel, by contrast, can never be known from conscience but must be revealed by God (8, cf. Pless, 12-13).

[18] In one sense, of course, God's standard of righteousness is not utilitarian – it simply *is*. But Luther correctly discerns the *effect* of this standard of righteousness – and that is what humans somewhat chauvinistically refer to as its "use" (its function from our perspective).

[19] Forde says that the law "exposes *sin* not just sins" and contends that the former may be understood to include "covetousness of virtue" and "the quest of self-salvation" (414). Also, "the law functions first and foremost . . . to reveal that apart from justification by faith there is no hope for us" (446). See Gerhard O. Forde, "Christian Life," in Carl Braaten and Robert Jensen, eds., *Christian Dogmatics* (Philadelphia: Fortress Press, 1984), 391-470.

[20] The connection between "two-fold use" and homiletics is especially emphasized by Lohse. See for example: "Luther distinguished various functions of the law and in this context spoke of a double *usus* (use). In doing so, he made clear terminologically that the distinction is to be related to preaching" (270).

[21] Among writers I have surveyed, only Lohse recognizes this terminological confusion. Almost as an aside, he indicates that when the "educative function" is in view, "it is better to speak of a commandment than of a law" (275). The function of a commandment *per se* is "announcement of the divine will" though in the process of serving this function, biblical commandments might simultaneously operate as *law*, i.e., in an "accusing" manner. So, I would add, might biblical promises, which also function primarily as announcements of the divine will.

[22] Forde, who handily rejects any "third use of the law," fails to distinguish between *the law* as God's standard of righteousness and "laws" as individual commandments. This is curious, because Forde makes much of the distinction between *sin* ("the quest for self-salvation") and sins ("our little failures") (414). Since he insists that *the law* serves to deal primarily with *sin*, it seems an obvious corollary that "laws" might therefore deal with "sins." Thus, the *law* referred to in Luther's formulation of Law and Gospel would have no so-called third use (on this Forde would be correct), but "laws" in the sense of individual commandments would be left to serve the catechetical, ethical function that has often been mislabeled "the third use of the law."

In contrast with Forde, Althaus insists that Luther *does* accept the third function of the law "in substance" even though he does not use the phrase (273). As proof of this, he says that "The Ten Commandments have their place not only 'before' but also 'after' justification; thus, they not only exercise the Christian in the theological function of the law but also lead him to a right knowledge of the good he ought to do according to God's will" (272). I note that Althaus here equates commandments (specifically, the Decalogue) with the *law* principle in Law and Gospel, though elsewhere he contends against such an identification (261).

Thus, we see how one mistake can produce two contrasting errors. On the one hand, the equation of commandments with *law* leads Althaus to ascribe to the law a function Luther denied it; he reasons that, since commandments obviously teach people God's will, that *must* be a function of the *law*. On the other hand, the equation of commandments with *law* leads Forde to decide that commandments cannot serve to teach people the will of God, since moral instruction is not one of the functions of *law*. But what if (as both Althaus and Forde sometimes know) *law* and "commandments" are not the same thing? Neither tenuous conclusion is necessary: The *law* has only the two functions Luther ascribed to it, while "commandments" (which are simply a genre of biblical literature) serve to do something else: They teach people the will of God (which is not a "third function of the law" but, rather, a "first function of commandments"). Of course, commandments like all genres of biblical literature might sometimes function as *law*, but they might also function as *gospel*, and in neither case is that function (as law or gospel) intrinsic to their genre or definitive of their purpose.

23 Althaus says that, for Luther, Jesus' Sermon on the Mount sharpened the demands of the law to the point that "sinful man . . . simply cannot fulfill it" (254; cf. *WA* 39, I, 364, 374).

24 Without being quite so cavalier, Forde dismisses Jesus' claim that all biblical commandments will remain until heaven and earth pass away (Matthew 5:17-18) by insisting that "'heaven and earth' *do* 'pass away' in the eschatological fulfillment anticipated and grasped by faith" (447). From an exegetical perspective this might be regarded as a desperate attempt to reconcile Matthew with Paul (specifically Romans 10:4). In a broader sense, Forde wants to reconcile the Matthean attitude toward commandments with the Lutheran concept of Law and Gospel. In either case, it is special pleading. A more helpful approach would be to recognize that Matthew probably means something different by "commandments" than either Paul or Luther meant by "law." But the root problem lies in trying to use the hermeneutical principle of Law and Gospel (concerned with the reception of texts) as an exegetical principle (to determine the intended meaning of texts).

25 Joachim Jeremias, *The Sermon on the Mount*, Facet Books (Philadelphia: Fortress Press, 1963).

26 Luther preferred to speak simply of "preaching Christ" which some (erroneously in my mind) have equated with "preaching gospel," i.e., with proclaiming the promises of grace and assurance that we have in Christ. But since Christ reveals God's holiness—in both his teaching and his person—we may say that Christ reveals the righteous standard of God that should be equated with *law* in the Lutheran formulation "law and gospel" as well as the affirmation of grace and mercy equated with *gospel*. In historical terms, according to Meuser, Luther himself experienced a learning curve in this regard (24). Early on, he stressed the promises and assurances of the gospel but later "when he saw people applying the assurances to themselves when they had no business doing so, this emphasis faded somewhat." But, still, the law remained a means or necessary step, not the end. "Unless the comfort and assurance of the gospel flooded the congregation, Luther felt that Christ had not been preached."

27 This, of course, does not mean that sermons have no element of instruction. According to Meuser, Luther typically viewed the sermon as "comprised of teaching and exhortation" (25). But, in practice, Meuser continues, "that's not the way Luther preached. He preached as if the sermon were not a classroom, but instead a battleground! Every sermon was a battle for the souls of the people."

28 It has also been an arena for debate over numerous questions, some of which are listed by Meuser: Are law and gospel always to be distinguished and kept separate? Are they enemies of one another? Is the law's function only to condemn? Must the

law always be preached prior to the gospel? Or is the law itself part of the gospel, itself an assurance? (22).

29 Reader-response criticism is often associated with either a) a postmodern hermeneutic that denies the stability and/or accessibility of meaning, and/or b) ideological approaches to texts (feminist, Marxist, etc.) that seek to impose lenses for understanding in ways that overtly reject or resist authorial intent. But, though reader-response criticism may be popular with scholars who operate with a postmodern or ideological hermeneutic, the approach itself assumes no particular epistemology. As a mode of literary analysis, reader response criticism simply employs various strategies for discerning anticipated effects of texts on various readers and identifying factors that make certain effects likely to be realized. See Mark Allan Powell, *Chasing the Eastern Star: Adventures in Biblical Reader-Response Criticism* (Louisville: Westminster John Knox Press, 2001).

30 Such an identification is, however, commonplace in Lutheranism. In an instruction book for those new to Lutheranism, Martin Marty says, "Law represents the demands of God, and the gospel is the promises of God." See Martin E. Marty, *Come and Grow with Us: New Member Basics* (Minneapolis: Augsburg Fortress Publishers, 1996), p. 10.

31 So Althaus: "For Luther, then, God's word can, in the final analysis, definitely not be categorized into law and gospel. The one and the same word strikes sinful man both as law and as gospel" (264). The functions of law and gospel "are functions of the same word. They always take place concurrently" (265). Also Lohse: "The distinction between law and gospel cannot be made once for all, but must be drawn ever anew . . . What is further unique about Luther's distinction is that law and gospel cannot be assigned to the Old or New Testament, nor to particular biblical passages, so as to establish for all time that one text is only law and the other gospel. Most texts assigned to the law have also a gospel side, and most texts assigned to the gospel have also a law side . . . Luther's distinction is clearly related to the context of proclamation" (269). Walther suggests that the choice of preaching law or gospel be determined by need of the audience: "The law is to be preached to secure sinners and the gospel to alarmed sinners" (17)—but it seems to me that most congregations may contain both types of sinners and that individual sinners may experience both security and alarm within the course of a single sermon.

32 Paulson says, "Law and gospel is thus not a *method* of preaching or interpretation . . . distinguishing law and gospel does not happen in the realm of doctrine or ideas or theology, it happens only when these words are given by a preacher to *you*" (40-41).

# APPENDIX 1
## Law and Gospel

### Lutheran principle of Law and Gospel

Lutherans say that the Word of God speaks both Law and Gospel, that these must be properly distinguished and yet also held together for God's Word to be fulfilled:

- Law = that which accuses us and judges us.
- Gospel = that which comforts us and saves us.

Faithful interpretation discerns Law and Gospel; faithful proclamation declares Law and Gospel.

### Two-fold (or three-fold) use of the law

Lutherans say that "the law" has two (or three) functions:

- the political function of maintaining some semblance of order in society.
- the theological function of showing us our need for the gospel.

And, maybe . . .

- the ethical or catechetical function of teaching us right from wrong.

### Two definitions of "the law"

1. God's standard of righteousness— the holy will of God in light of which all human endeavors are judged

2. A genre of biblical literature— commandments and other materials that relate how God wants people to live

---

**Function of the law: An integrated paradigm**

1. **Law defined as "God's standard of righteousness, the holy will of God"** has only two functions:
   - To maintain a semblance of order in society·
   - To show us our need for the gospel

2. **Law defined as "biblical commandments and related literature"** has one function:
   - To teach us right from wrong

**Law and Gospel is a hermeneutical principle, not an exegetical one.**

Exegesis deals with the narrow task of interpretation—discerning the meaning of biblical texts. Hermeneutics deals with the broader question of considering what is meant by being "faithful to Scripture" once it has been interpreted

The task of exegesis is to consider texts within their historical and literary contexts and determine the meaning that each text was intended to have. We ought not assume that every text was intended to speak either a word of judgment or a word of salvation. Specifically, the primary meaning of Torah as determined by exegesis would not be "to show people their need of the gospel," but, hermeneutically, we might identify this as an inevitable consequence of receiving Torah as the words of a holy God spoken to sinful humanity. So, the hermeneutical principle of Law and Gospel becomes a tool for discerning the ultimate effect of Scripture.

**Law and Gospel is primarily a homiletical principle.**

The ELCA Constitution speaks of God's Word in a three-fold sense: the Incarnate Word (Jesus Christ himself), the Proclaimed Word (the message of Law and Gospel), and the Written Word (the Bible). Law and Gospel applies mainly and most importantly to the proclaimed word, to preaching.

Preaching is different from teaching in Lutheran homiletical tradition. The sermon is not viewed as part of the church's educational ministry but as part of its liturgy. A sermon is a liturgical act that serves as a means of grace, conveying Law and Gospel to people. The goal of a sermon is not to provide people with doctrinal or moral instruction. It is to proclaim God's word that judges or accuses and God's word that comforts or saves. Naturally, such a concept affects the way we interpret Scripture for the task of preaching. But Law and Gospel is a homiletical principle that would not govern all interpretation of Scripture for purposes other than preaching.

**Law and Gospel assumes a reader-oriented approach to Scripture.**

The categories of "law" and "gospel" must be defined in terms of effect on the recipient, not in terms of intrinsic content or even with reference to authorial intent. They define the effects of Scripture: The Word of God judges, accuses, comforts, saves.

**Summary of exegetical, hermeneutical, homiletical process.**

Scripture may be faithfully exegeted so as to reveal the basic intentions of its original author. From this, we may discern a plurality of possible effects that the text might have on people in various contexts, effects that would be congruent with authorial intent even if they go beyond the specifics of such intent. And from that plurality of potential effects, the Lutheran preacher should be encouraged to select two—the accusatory effect of law and the comforting effect of gospel.

# Interpret Boldly
## *Lutherans Reading the Bible*[1]

### Esther Menn
*Lutheran School of Theology at Chicago*

Biblical interpretation today is for the most part broadly ecumenical, even interfaith, in its methods and insights. In my own life, I have studied and taught the Bible in a variety of contexts—with women, men, youth, and children of different ages from a variety of Christian denominational backgrounds, as well as with a number of Muslims and Jews. As a biblical scholar who has been a Lutheran from birth, I found the occasion of this Hein-Fry lecture to be a challenging opportunity to consider what might be distinctive about Lutheran biblical interpretation.

As a starting point, I would emphasize that Lutherans affirm the power of God's Word. By the Word, Lutherans do not simply mean the words that appear on the pages of the written Bible. The Word includes the multiple ways that God is active in the world: through Christ; through our witness to each other in preaching, service, fellowship, and other forms of mutual ministry; and through the holy Scriptures that lead us to faith.[2] The Word of God in the Bible continues to address us in our own contexts in the twenty-first century, even as we recognize that these same Scriptures have also addressed other audiences in ancient times and that they continue to address other communities in our contemporary world, including the Jewish community with their own traditions of interpreting the Hebrew scriptures.

As evangelicals, Lutherans also affirm that in the Bible we encounter the good news of the gospel, which meets us where we are to liberate and transform us. The gospel message of the Bible is "God's good news for our bad situations," to quote Lutheran Old Testament scholar Ralph

Klein in a recent Lutheran Heritage Lecture at the Lutheran School of Theology at Chicago.[3]

In addition to these basic convictions, which many if not most Christians would affirm, there are more specifically Lutheran themes and guiding principles that inform Lutheran biblical interpretation. Well-known formulations such as the following spring immediately to mind: the theology of the cross, the Bible as the manger of the Christ child, Law and Gospel, and justification by faith alone.

These phrases summarize precious Lutheran theological insights that frame our interpretation of the Bible and indeed our whole theological outlook as Lutherans. How to move from these Lutheran shibboleths to specific biblical texts, in all their variety and richness, can be a perplexing question, however. It may take a case study to get deeper into this matter of Lutheran biblical interpretation.

For this purpose, I have chosen 2 Kings 5:1-19, commonly understood as the story of Naaman's healing[4] (although I would argue that Naaman's conversion to exclusive worship of the God of Israel is the climax of the narrative). The first fourteen verses of this narrative appear as a first lesson in the Revised Common Lectionary, which we read every third year in the context of a Sunday worship service. The selection of this case study points to some additional observations about Lutheran biblical interpretation. One is that for Lutherans the holy Scriptures include the Old Testament as well as the New Testament. Martin Luther was what we would now call an Old Testament professor at the University of Wittenberg, and he valued the first part of the Christian canon immensely. In fact, in one of his characteristically challenging statements, Luther ventured that if the Jewish scriptures had been correctly interpreted, there would have been no need for the New Testament, which was originally not written Scripture at all, but rather oral proclamation about Christ.[5]

Another observation arising from this selection of a lesson from the Revised Common Lectionary is that biblical texts play a central role in Lutheran worship. Related to this fact is the prominence of preaching from lectionary texts as one of the most important forms of interpretation within Lutheran congregations. None of these additional observations is exclusively Lutheran either, but rather ecumenically Christian.

Similarly, the methods that I will use to interpret 2 Kings 5:1-19 are not distinctively Lutheran, but rather draw on the broader scholarly field of biblical studies. My interpretation will employ literary criticism, insights and sensitivities from feminism, and the lens of the child (paying attention to an almost invisible child character), as well as theological and ideological criticism.

After looking closely at this text and discerning how it communicates its message of good news, there will be an opportunity to return to the question of Lutheran biblical interpretation, asking in retrospect the questions: How Lutheran was this interpretation of 2 Kings 5:1-19? What exactly makes it Lutheran? And what might make it even more Lutheran? I will then take the opportunity to explore and analyze how Martin Luther himself interpreted the narrative in 2 Kings 5. Finally I will conclude with a parting encouragement about Lutheran biblical interpretation in these times.

In order to place the selected biblical text before us, I will quote 2 Kings 5:1-19a in full from the New Revised Standard Version:

> 1 Naaman, commander of the army of the king of Aram, was a great man and in high favor with his master, because by him the LORD had given victory to Aram. The man, though a mighty warrior, suffered from leprosy. 2 Now the Arameans on one of their raids had taken a young girl captive from the land of Israel, and she served Naaman's wife. 3 She said to her mistress, "If only my lord were before the prophet who is in Samaria! He would cure him of his leprosy." 4 So Naaman went in and told his lord just what the girl from the land of Israel had said. 5 And the king of Aram said, "Go, then, and I will send along a letter to the king of Israel."
>
> He went, taking with him ten talents of silver, six thousand shekels of gold, and ten sets of garments.    6 He brought the letter to the king of Israel, which read, "When this letter reaches you, know that I have sent to you my servant Naaman, that you may cure him of his leprosy." 7 When the king of Israel read the letter, he tore his clothes and said, "Am I God, to give death or life, that this man sends word to me to cure a man of his leprosy? Just look and see how he is trying to pick a quarrel with me!"

8 But when Elisha the man of God heard that the king of Israel had torn his clothes, he sent a message to the king, "Why have you torn your clothes? Let him come to me, that he may learn that there is a prophet in Israel." 9 So Naaman came with his horses and chariots, and halted at the entrance of Elisha's house. 10 Elisha sent a messenger to him, saying, "Go, wash in the Jordan seven times, and your flesh shall be restored and you shall be clean. 11 But Naaman became angry and went away, saying, "I thought that for me he would surely come out, and stand and call on the name of the Lord his God, and would wave his hand over the spot, and cure the leprosy! 12 Are not Abana and Pharpar, the rivers of Damascus, better than all the waters of Israel? Could I not wash in them, and be clean?" He turned and went away in a rage. 13 But his servants approached and said to him, "Father, if the prophet had commanded you to do something difficult, would you not have done it? How much more, when all he said to you was, 'Wash, and be clean'?" 14 So he went down and immersed himself seven times in the Jordan, according to the word of the man of God; his flesh was restored like the flesh of a young boy, and he was clean.

15 Then he returned to the man of God, he and all his company; he came and stood before him and said, "Now I know that there is no God in all the earth except in Israel; please accept a present from your servant." 16 But he said, "As the Lord lives, whom I serve, I will accept nothing!" He urged him to accept, but he refused. 17 Then Naaman said, "If not, please let two mule-loads of earth be given to your servant; for your servant will no longer offer burnt offering or sacrifice to any god except the Lord. 18 But may the Lord pardon your servant on one count: when my master goes into the house of Rimmon to worship there, leaning on my arm, and I bow down in the house of Rimmon, when I do bow down in the house of Rimmon, may the Lord pardon your servant on this one count." 19 He said to him, "Go in peace." [6]

## Lens of the Child

To read this narrative of Namaan's healing and conversion through the lens of the child character that appears briefly at its beginning is in some ways counterintuitive. The little girl captured from the land of Israel who serves the wife of Naaman, the commander of the army of Aram (also known as Syria), is a minor character who would be very easy to overlook. Her role is so small that she has no name, and she never reappears as an adult later in the narrative of Israel's history. Yet, this child plays an inspirational and pivotal role.

The biblical narrative depicts her suggesting a solution to a difficult problem, intervening when adults are threatened and ineffectual, offering theological insights into God's ways, and acting within the context of international conflict between cultures and national identities. These are complex and surprising contributions to the story by one so young and seemingly unimportant. To ignore this child would be insensitive to the dynamics of the biblical narrative.

In our own context in the twenty-first century, moreover, to overlook this child in our interpretation might be more than insensitive. It would even be dangerous, since it would mimic a common tendency to discount children as less than fully human and not entirely worth respect as bearing the image of God. In our time, we need to pay renewed attention to children, who are always the most vulnerable members of any community and are becoming ever more vulnerable and threatened, as we continue to experience the global economic, political, and environmental crises of our age.

## The Little Israelite Girl

The child character that we meet in this passage lives during a time of war, making her context similar to our own period of armed conflict over borders, security, resources, and other matters.[7] The nation of Aram was Israel's greatest enemy during the reign of the Omride kings in the ninth century BCE. According to the biblical story, Israel's own God gave victory to the Arameans through the leadership of Naaman (2 Kings 5:1).

Yet despite Naaman's greatness as a military strategist and mighty warrior, he suffers from leprosy. This skin condition, which is not Hanson's disease or what we call leprosy today, but perhaps psoriasis, eczema, acne, or some other affliction of the skin, was of such concern that two whole chapters are devoted to it in Leviticus (Leviticus 13-14). It is ironic that Naaman's name in Hebrew means "pleasant," which accords with his success in life, but contrasts with the misery of his leprous condition.

Unexpectedly, the little Israelite girl comes forward to identify to her mistress a source of healing for Naaman's skin disease. She said to her mistress, "If only my lord were with the prophet who is in Samaria! He would cure him of his leprosy" (2 Kings 5:3).

From a feminist perspective, it is worth note that the identification of a cure occurs within a conversation between the two female characters in this narrative, each from a different side of the battle line. It is within this relationship between women that individuals from different ethnic backgrounds speak to each other as human beings. Their relationship is a hierarchical one, however, far from equality, and this never changes in this story. The Hebrew text describes the little girl as being "before" (*lifne*) Naaman's wife, an expression indicating her subordinate position that the NRSV paraphrases by asserting that "she served Naaman's wife."

In light of this power relationship, something more than meets the eye may be at stake. We might ask why these female characters are speaking about Naaman's leprosy, which we can imagine he would have hidden to all but his most intimate of companions. We might read this narrative as a "text of terror," to use the phrase of Phyllis Trible.[8] Did Naaman's leprosy cause his wife to reject him from her bed and to supply him with another sexual companion in the person of this Israelite girl? (One thinks in these days of the expectation in some parts of the world, such as regions of India or Africa, that intercourse with a virgin will cure a man of HIV/AIDS.) The sexual use of female captives of war is treated as a commonplace practice in a number of other biblical passages (Deuteronomy 23:10-14; Judges 5:30; 21:8-23).

The text in 2 Kings remains silent on such matters, even though it is suggestive. Whatever the case, it is in the face to face conversation between these two female characters that a way forward to Naaman's cure is identified. While neither the Israelite girl nor her Syrian mistress remain long in the narrative focus which is dominated by men, their communication sets the ensuing narrative in motion and foreshadows its outcome.

Immediately after Naaman reports the little girl's words to the king of Aram, this king responds by sending his leprous commander to the

Israelite king in Samaria with rich payments and a document demanding healing. The king of Israel despairs because of his inability to comply with such an impossible request, which he takes as a provocation to further battle, until the prophet Elisha comes forward to remedy the situation.[9] Elisha's simple cure of dipping seven times into the Jordan initially insults Naaman, but his healing is immediate once he complies. Naaman then acknowledges Israel's God as the only God "in all the earth" (2 Kings 5:15) and makes arrangements to bring back a cartload of earth from Israel upon which to offer his burnt offerings to the Lord, even from his home in Aram (2 Kings 5:17).

## Valuing Things Big and Small

It is striking that the nameless little Israelite girl appears in only three verses (2 Kings 5:2-4) of the story of Naaman's healing and conversion to the worship of the Lord, the God of Israel (2 Kings. 5:1-19). In her minor role, she has only one brief appearance and one spoken line. The girl's small role matches her insignificance as a spoil of war and a house servant for the wife of the commander who defeated her people. Her marginality as a child captive enslaved in enemy territory represents the weakness of the northern kingdom of Israel, which was unable to protect her and no doubt many others like her in time of war. Yet, in her vulnerability as a captive in a foreign land, the little girl's words challenge the pretensions of the mighty and offer hope for healing and life.

This narrative presents a sustained contrast between what appears "big" and important and what appears "small" and insignificant, that ultimately inverts their usual valuation. Naaman, the commander of the army of the king of Aram is introduced up front as a "big man" (*'ish gadol*, 2 Kings 5:1, translated as a "great man" in the NRSV), whereas the child captive from Israel with no name is described as a "little girl" (*na'arah qetannah*, 2 Kings 5:2, translated as a "young girl" in the NRSV) in the following verse.[10] This initial contrast between size and gender accentuates the small female child's placement within world events dominated by men, involving armies and kings, commanders and prophets. In the big world into which the conflict between Israel and Syria has forced her as an enslaved captive of war, the girl child is introduced simply as "little," as if that is the one thing that matters—her smallness in the midst of everything mighty, powerful, and overwhelming.

As the story progresses, we find other remarkable uses of the adjectives "big" and "little." When Naaman balks at the simple instructions that Elisha gives through a messenger, his servants note that if the prophet had given him a "big" task to do (Hebrew, *davar gadol*, 2 Kings 5:13, translated as something "difficult" in the NRSV), he would have simply done it. A "big" demand from the prophet would have been in keeping with Naaman's important status as a "big" man (2 Kings 5:1). His servants' observation overcomes Naaman's resistance to washing in the waters of the Jordan, which initially seem much less to him than the waters of the Abana and the Pharpar rivers flowing through Damascus (2 Kings 5:12). After he dips in the Jordan, Naaman's flesh is restored, like the flesh of a "little boy" (*na'ar qaton*, 2 Kings 5:14, translated as a "young boy" in the NRSV). Naaman becomes like the "little girl" at the beginning of the story in his pure flesh and also ultimately in his recognition of the God of Israel who works for healing through the prophet in Samaria (2 Kings 5:15-18).

## The Power of a Wish

What is "little" in this narrative is certainly not to be dismissed. As the narrative spotlight turns to the little Israelite girl for the briefest moment, the display of everything grand and significant in the world of war suddenly comes to a halt. Although she is small and lacks any official power, the girl's few words are the first spoken in the narrative. All subsequent action of the more prominent characters hinge on them, so they are worth repeating:

She said to her mistress, "If only my lord were with (*lifne*) the prophet who is in Samaria! He would cure him of his leprosy" (2 Kings 5:3).

What kind of words does the little girl offer to Naaman's wife? Her single line contains no lament or complaint, no whining or cursing, all of which we might expect from a diminutive captive of war forced to serve the enemy. Her words are also not a command nor a report, nor any other kind of speech that would have its place in times of war and in the high circles that manage war. Instead, the little girl's words express a wish contrary to fact: "if only" (*'ahale*, 2 Kings 5:3). The girl has a heart full of compassion and wishes only for the enemy commander's healing, despite his role in defeating her people and taking her into captivity. She also wants to make known and share the power for life which is among her own people, through the prophet in Samaria. We sense the ethnic pride in her words. But even more remarkable in a time of killing and destruction, the girl focuses her attention on healing and restoration, even for the military leader on the other side.

The little girl no doubt wishes that many things were different. We can imagine that she would certainly like to be at home, to be with her parents and neighbors and country people. But the only words that we have in this story express her wish that Naaman could be with (*lifne*) the prophet in Samaria. Simple presence is what she wishes for Naaman, just as proximity and immediacy are what children want most from their parents and others whom they love and trust to make things right. Her words express confidence that this kind of closeness to the prophet would lead to Naaman's healing.

The words that the little girl speaks suggest a childlike, indiscriminate hope that things might be better for everyone, everywhere. Her wish envisions a world without sharply drawn national borders and without clear-cut divisions between enemies and friends. Her words lack rancor or resentment for what has happened to disrupt her life. They are a magnanimous expression of trust that there is a force for life and healing more powerful than any army. If only the power of healing and life possessed by the prophet in Samaria were the power that was recognized and respected in international relations.

## From Wish to International Crisis

The information about the healing power of the prophet at Samaria presented in the little girl's wish causes something of an international crisis when it falls into the hands of the military leader Naaman and his superior, the king of Aram. These important adults take a child's wish and attempt to turn it into an economic and political transaction, as if impressive amounts of silver, gold, and expensive garments could buy the healing that the little girl's words locate in enemy territory. The adults also bully a child's wish into a command, and not only a verbal command, but a formal, written command, carried in a letter by none other than the leprous leader of the Aramean army himself.

Although the Aramean king demands that the king of Israel perform a healing for his leprous commander, the power of healing is not the power of kings. Their area of expertise is war, killing, and death. To his credit, the king of Israel realizes that the power to restore the health of a leper belongs to God alone. He tears his clothes as a sign of mourning and extreme distress, and asks: "Am I God, to give death or life, that this man sends word to me to cure a man of his leprosy?" (2 Kings. 5:7).

But even though the king of Israel recognizes God as the source of all healing and even though he acknowledges that he is not God, he still is unable to see the real human need that the enemy commander embodies in his leprous flesh. The king panics because he cannot see behind this clumsy international pressure a sincere desire for health, and he cannot see the common humanity that he shares with his enemy. He can only conclude that it must be a pretext for more conflict: "Just look and see how he is trying to pick a quarrel with me" (2 Kings 5:7). The crisis in the palace in Samaria indicates a fear that the enemy's search for wholeness is only another cause for violence and killing, a prelude to further defeat. The little girl's wish for the enemy's health becomes in the king's palace an impossible order, an international crisis, and a security threat.

By contrast, the little girl was able to see the humanity of the Aramean general, his basic frailty and mortality, even though he was so great a man. She also pointed to the power of God's prophet in Samaria. The Prophet Elisha himself similarly desires to show Naaman that there is a prophet in Israel through his healing, as he tells the Israelite king: "Let [Naaman] come to me, that he may know that there is a prophet in Israel" (2 Kings 5:8). Elisha's words confirm that the little girl spoke the truth when she located the power of healing in the prophet in Samaria.

The role of the prophet in healing is entirely overlooked in the international crisis caused by the search for Naaman's cure. The Aramean king demands that the Israelite king heal his leprous commander, and the Israelite king knows that he does not have that power. But neither of these nameless royal figures, nor Naaman himself, acting as a messenger conveying the order for his own healing, remembers the little girl's wish that the military commander could be with the prophet in Samaria (2 Kings 5:3), nor do they seem to comprehend that the power of healing lies with God through the prophet's mediation (2 Kings 5:8).

# Conjuring the Prophet

It is not within the power of kings to command the prophets who have their independent source of authority through their direct relationship to God, through their roles as spokesperson, intercessor, and conduit of divine power, including the power to heal. The Prophet Elisha is not summoned by the king in Samaria, but rather he suddenly emerges in the narrative to send his own message to the king (2 Kings 5:8). Elisha becomes involved in the situation once the Israelite king acknowledges his own weakness and impotence by rending his garments. Elisha acts to bring the focus back on the role of the prophet, which is exactly what the little girl had stressed in her wish for her master.

Elisha summons Naaman to his home, but then declines to meet the commander personally when he arrives with his horses and chariots, in a display of military might and political importance (2 Kings 5:8-10). Naaman does not get the big fanfare that he no doubt expected. Nor does he receive the healing ritual or the "big" therapeutic protocol that he anticipated (2 Kings 5:11). The prescription is simply to dip seven times in the Jordan (2 Kings 5:10). This modest regimen in a river of only minor significance is in keeping with the theme of the power of small things, exemplified also in the power of the "little" girl to recognize the healing gift of the prophet in Samaria.

The first time that we hear Naaman speak in this story is to express his irritation with the lack of respect shown to him and with the disregard shown to the great rivers of his home country. Naaman is angry that he is not treated as the "big," important man that he is, that the prophet does not officially welcome and acknowledge him as powerful and worthy of a private audience. He resents that the standard therapeutic treatment he had expected was withheld (2 Kings 5:11). He is also offended about the commonness of the means of healing that the prophet identifies, since the Jordan is insignificant in comparison with the larger rivers of Damascus, the Abana and the Pharpar (2 Kings. 5:12).

It is the lowly servants who are able to point Naaman towards compliance with the lowly instruction of the prophet. Once again, as in the case of the little Israelite servant girl, it is those in a subordinate position who articulate the truth and move the narrative toward healing and life. The servants' perspective and function are similar to that of the little girl.

They diplomatically observe that if their "father" had been given a difficult task, some "big thing" (*davar gadol*, 2 Kings 5:13) to do, he would have done it immediately. The commander is used to mounting major operations, to moving large companies, to bearing up under strain and duress, in order to wield war's power of destruction and death. He seems incapable of accepting a small assignment for the sake of health and life.

Once Naaman does acquiesce to being treated as a person of no special consequence, as less like a "father" and more like a child vulnerable to being summarily discounted, once he acknowledges the modest river of the Jordan as a potential means of healing and dips in the river seven times, he is cured immediately, and his skin becomes like that of a little boy (*na'ar qaton*, 2 Kings 5:14). This comparison of course emphasizes the complete healing of his skin, since there is no finer and more beautiful skin than the skin of a child, without blemish, even in tone and in texture, with quick healing properties. In this context, where the "little girl" wished her master good health, it also seems significant that as soon as he taps into the power for healing that she articulated, he himself becomes childlike. He becomes a "little boy," the counterpart of the "little girl," at least skin deep.

Here is where the Revised Common Lectionary reading ends, with Naaman's restoration to health, perhaps to create a closer correspondence with the narrative structure of the Gospel reading for the day, which is Mark 1:40-45, telling of Jesus' healing of a leper. But the story initiated by the little Israelite girl and her wish continues. To stop at this point would eliminate some of the important structural components of this particular narrative, which surprisingly throw the focus back on the little girl who appears at its beginning.

## Dirt and Worship

The mighty Naaman becomes a worshipper of Israel's God through his experience of the power of small things. He attended to what the little girl said; he was healed through simple, repetitive contact with the humble Jordan; and his skin was transformed from leprous to that of a little boy. Naaman's reaction to the effectiveness of what appears insignificant is to return with the rest of his company to stand "before" (*lifne*) the man of God who restored his flesh (2 Kings 5:15). This action at last fulfils the little girl's wish that her master were "before" (*lifne*) this prophet in Samaria (2 Kings 5:3).

In Hebrew to stand "before" (*lifne*) someone can imply more than bodily placement. It can indicate acknowledgment of the authority of a superior. At the beginning of the story, Naaman was an important man "before" (*lifne*) his master, the king of Aram (2 Kings 5:1), and the little girl captured from Israel appeared "before" (*lifne*) Naaman's wife (2 Kings 5:2), who appears to be her mistress.[11] So now, finally, Naaman stands "before" (*lifne*) the man of God (2 Kings 5:15; cf., 2 Kings 5:3), recognizing the saving authority of the prophet in Samaria. Elisha his healer in turn stands "before" (*lifne*) the LORD (2 Kings 5:16), whom Naaman now also recognizes as the only God.

Naaman urges Elisha to accept a reward (2 Kings 5:15-16), but the prophet's refusal reveals that the economy of healing is distinct from the plunder of kings and armies. If we were to continue to the end of the chapter, (2 Kings 5:19-27), we would learn of the negative consequences of entangling the prophet's vocation with material transactions. Elisha's servant Gehazi secretively claims a reduced payment of two changes of clothes from Naaman, but as a result he himself becomes afflicted with Naaman's leprosy, thus reopening the story plot of a need for healing at its conclusion.

Since Naaman cannot give anything, he requests instead to take something for himself. He plans to take back a load of soil from Israel, in keeping with the understanding that each land had its own deity who was worshiped in that particular territory. Naaman's mule-cart load of earth seems like a small gesture, but it is symbolic of his total allegiance. At the end of the narrative, the big Syrian commander and the little girl from Israel recognize the same God.

The Israelite girl living on foreign soil testified to the power of healing that Israel's God offers through the "man of God" (2 Kings 5:15) living in Samaria. Her witness in a foreign land started a whole string of events that led finally to the Syrian captain's healing and to his acknowledgment of his enemies' deity while visiting their capital city of Samaria. The little girl had wished something good for the foreign enemy of her people, and now this enemy has become a fellow worshipper of the LORD, the God of Israel, and no other gods (2 Kings 5:17).

Instead of the usual spoils of war, including captive children to serve as slaves and wives, Naaman takes home dirt. He carries back a bit of earth from Israel upon which he plans to sacrifice to the Lord, the God of Israel (2 Kings 5:17), whom he acknowledges as God over all the earth, even if upon occasion he must accompany the king of Aram in his official worship of the Aramean god Rimmon (2 Kings 5:18).

As he seems to have made the little girl a servant through war, so Naaman makes himself a servant on foreign soil. Describing his plans to bring home a cartload of earth, the army commander repeatedly calls himself the "servant" or even "slave" (*'eved*, 2 Kings 5:15, 17, 18, which can be translated either as "servant" or "slave") of Elisha, the prophet of Israel's God who healed him of his leprosy. Naaman's self-description as a "servant" appears a total of five times in this passage (once in 2 Kings 5:15, twice in 2 Kings 5:17 and in 2 Kings. 5:18). By striking contrast, it should be noted that although it is implied that the little girl is under her mistress's authority when it states she was "before" (*lifne*) Naaman's wife (2 Kings 5:2, paraphrased as "she served Naaman's wife" in the NRSV), she is never once explicitly called a "servant" in the biblical text.

In light of the narrator's acknowledgement that Israel's God was acting beyond the borders of Israel in giving victory to Aram through Naaman (2 Kings 5:1), this act of transporting dirt in order to be able to worship the Lord outside of the land seems superfluous. Elisha neither condones nor condemns Naaman's intentions, but only sends the great enemy warrior home in "health" and "peace," which are both possible translations of the Hebrew word *shalom*. Elisha's parting blessing, which may be translated literally, "Walk towards health and peace" (2 Kings 5:19) is a most ironic and significant conclusion to this narrative set within the context of illness and war. The man of God in Samaria upsets human expectations by setting forth God's values for abundant life.

## Mercy and Embrace

This biblical narrative mocks the apparent power of the mighty and exalted, of kings and commanders. It qualifies the effectiveness of war and wealth in the things that really matter. At the same time, it is a story of deep mercy and embrace. No one is cast out into the outer darkness where there is eternal gnashing of teeth. In the end, even the most powerful enemy is healed and transformed into one who recognizes and worships

Israel's God. Naaman himself stutteringly acknowledges that he depends on God's forgiveness as he moves into a future full of ambiguities and conflicts of interest (1 Kings 5:18).

From the start of the narrative, the little girl from Israel offers insight into who holds true power over health and life. She intervenes to identify a solution to a problem that confounds adults and threatens life. She witnesses to the source of healing for the powerful commander of the Syrian army, in the prophet who is in Samaria. Her leadership is acknowledged by the adult characters of the narrative, as they take action based on her words.

The little Israelite girl expresses theological insight and witnesses to her faith. Her words confirm that God is active in the narrative, even among the Arameans, the enemy of her own people. This child's testimony is central to the story and expresses a particular understanding of the community's relationship with God, especially as mediated by the figure of the prophet in Samaria. She testifies to God's power over all life, through her wish that initiates Naaman's quest for health and eventually leads to the even bigger step of his acknowledging Israel's God as the only God in all the earth.

Remarkably, the story also portrays a child acting on the borders between cultures and national identities, negotiating divides that sometimes baffle and hobble older people. Her words initiate the crossing of national boundaries in search of the good gifts of healing and life, even during a time of war when power generally means the ability to kill and defeat and establish new borders to be defended. The Israelite girl is depicted not as an isolated and protected minor, but as an effective actor embedded within complex social and international structures and relationships. She acts with compassion and kindness not simply to a stranger and a foreigner, but even to her people's enemy.

Although the little Israelite girl is an agent of change and hope amidst international conflict, her story also illustrates children's vulnerability and marginalization. She is tragically and permanently separated from her family and her community, as a captive of war now serving the wife of the enemy commander. Her isolation and subordinate position would also leave her open to sexual exploitation, rape, and abuse by an aggressive male head of household who is used to exercising power. The girl's story points to the precarious situation of children of all ages, who are too often caught in the violence and upset of communal or national conflicts.

Interpreting this biblical narrative through the lens of the little Israelite girl shows that God is at work in families, communities, and nations not only through the mighty and the powerful by human standards, but also through the weak and insignificant. It is "not by might, nor by power, but by my spirit, says the LORD of hosts" (Zechariah 4:6). God's spirit is surprisingly present and active through what might appear to be weakness, vulnerability, and trust that this child represents so well.

## A Gospel Story

The story of the little Israelite girl may be considered a "gospel" story, in that it reveals God's good news for our bad situations. It shows how out of the context of war and displacement, in a position of vulnerability and weakness, a captive female child, from a defeated country, the least of the least, is able to preserve insight, empathy, and faith, leading to the healing and conversion of the Syrian commander. This story claims that the power of war and destruction are not the final word. It reveals that God provides another economy of healing and life, embracing even enemies who are sent forth cured and in peace.

This story asserts that children have value, although they are small and vulnerable, and becoming more and more vulnerable today, to poverty, abuse, neglect, broken families, dysfunctional communities, prisons, drive-by shootings, failed schools, sex trafficking, racial discrimination, lack of health care, lack of economic opportunities, gangs, illegal drugs, conscription as child soldiers, suicide, and despair.

To bring more specificity to this discussion, in a written communication from March 2009, John Nunes, CEO and president of Lutheran Word Relief (and concurrently a doctoral candidate at LSTC), emphasized the severity of the impact the current economic crisis has on children. He quoted Nicholas Kristoff, in a *New York Times* column, who "cautions us against focusing too sharply on our own economic woes here in the U.S. 'It's worth remembering,' [Kristoff] says, 'that the consequence of a deep recession in a poor country isn't just a lost job but also a lost child.'[12] Children are indeed dying as a consequence of today's global economic woes. The World Bank estimates that the global market meltdown means that every hour, an additional twenty-two children are dying in the world's poorest countries—that's over and above the ten million children under five who already die each year from hunger-related causes."

This story offers us a vision of how God is acting in the world and it invites us to recognize anew that as the body of Christ we are called and empowered to live out the values of healing, mercy, and peace. The fact that the little girl is not freed in this story, that her fate is not revealed or yet determined at its conclusion, challenges us to realize that we live in a broken world and that there is still much work to be done. There remains an urgent need for concern, involvement, and deliverance, and Scripture opens our eyes and hearts to acknowledge what might be easy for us to overlook. What does it mean for us today that children are malnourished, abused, neglected, and otherwise needing our attention, when we know that God cares for them? In my opinion, Lutheran World Relief and Lutheran Social Service may be considered to be practical instances of Lutheran biblical interpretation, in that these agencies embody our commitment to respond to God's grace and bounty made known through the Scriptures, including through this story in 2 Kings 5:1-19.

And if all this is not enough, 2 Kings 5:1-19 is a delightful and whimsical story that conveys all of these points through humor and gentle surprise—not through heavy-handed polemics or diatribes. It elevates the spirit and leaves us open and primed to recognize God's unexpected grace, healing, and peace in the tumult of our own lives, families, and communities. The Prophet Elisha's parting blessing, which is anticipated by the little Israelite girl's wish, may be extended to us all: "Walk towards health and peace" (2 Kings 5:19).

## Lutheran Lenses

Interpreting 2 Kings 5:1-19 as an Old Testament "gospel story" by highlighting the good news of God's presence in a broken world certainly fits within a Lutheran framework, although this interpretation would also be compatible with other Christian denominational perspectives as well. One might press further to explore how this story might look through some of the classic Lutheran theological lenses listed in the introductory remarks, although time permits only a cursory exploration of a few of the possibilities.

If we consider the words of the Bible as not identical letter for letter with God's Word but, as Luther expressed it, holding that Word as the manger or swaddling clothes that held the Christ child at his birth, then perhaps we have done well to concentrate on the child in this story. Luther's incarnational, sacramental theology of Scripture draws a metaphor from the Christmas narrative in Luke's gospel (Luke 2:7), but in this particular case the imagery of the Christ child might sharpen the focus on another real child, the little Israelite girl in 2 Kings 5, who like Jesus in the stable occupies a most humble and vulnerable station.

Luther contended that, properly understood, all Scripture is about Christ, in that it proclaims Christ and leads to faith. From this perspective, we might understand the little girl as a Christ-figure in this story. She proclaims the Word of God's healing, both to the characters in this narrative and also to us, who similarly need to hear this message of God's active presence even in a war-ravaged and disease-threatened world. The Revised Common Lectionary, by pairing this narrative in 2 Kings with a story in the gospel of Mark about Jesus' healing of a leper (Mark 1:40-45), suggests that this Old Testament lesson points forward to Jesus' power to heal. In turn, Jesus' concern for the leper imparts christological significance to the little girl's similar concern.

If attention shifts too soon to apparent parallels with the New Testament in an attempt to identify Christ in the manger and swaddling clothing of Scripture, however, the specifics of the Old Testament story and its distinctive witness might be lost. In 2 Kings, the person with the primary role in Naaman's healing is actually Elisha, not the little girl who identifies the prophet in Samaria as the source of healing. But development of this closer correspondence between the roles of Elisha and Jesus as healers in a christological reading of the story could entirely eclipse the little girl and her compassionate wish. Even though the little girl appears to be a minor character, still her witness from the margins matters, and her words frame and structure the entire narrative, as shown in the preceding pages. While Christ will always remain central for Christian faith, Lutherans need to grant Old Testament texts their own integrity and hear their distinctive witness.

Taking up a theology of the cross as our Lutheran lens would accentuate the suffering in the narrative, both that of the girl war captive and that of Naaman. It would emphasize the paradox of God's presence in the world precisely out of the context of human brokenness and despair. From my perspective, this would perhaps be the place with the most potential to further develop a Lutheran reading of this story. We would need to explore further where God is in this story. The opening verse portrays God as bringing about the victory of the Arameans over the Israelites (2 Kings 5:1), which may suggest that God also caused or allowed the capture of the little girl. But the idea that God desires the little girl's suffering is theologically offensive and objectionable. What does seem clear is that God's absence in the little girl's captivity is also the very place that God's presence is made known, in her witness to life and healing from the context of her own despair. When compared to this gently humorous and whimsical story, however, the passion narratives impart quite a different substance and tone. Once again, this particular Lutheran lens of the cross both highlights aspects of the story that might otherwise be overlooked and, at the same time, threatens to overwhelm or distort this text's distinctive witness.

Law and Gospel has emerged as a classic Lutheran dialectic for interpreting the Scriptures, especially through preaching, but this signature Lutheran lens often leaves me perplexed, and certainly it does so in the case of this narrative. If by "law" Lutherans simply mean "our bad situations," such as war and disease, then certainly this story may be seen as in this light, but what then is the specific value of the concept "law" drawn from the legal context in that case? Why not speak more specifically of human vulnerability, hubris, dilemma, or mortality?

More generally, the pair of Law and Gospel is difficult for me as a biblical scholar, even a Lutheran biblical scholar, since "law" is a translation of the Hebrew "Torah," which actually means "teaching" or "revealed instruction" for life and blessing in a covenant relationship with God. The Hebrew Scriptures hold the Torah in highest esteem, as a source of life and delight, As Psalm 119 says, "Oh, how I love your Torah! It is my meditation all day long.... How sweet are your words to my taste, sweeter than honey to my mouth!" (Psalm 119:97, 103). Especially in the context of interfaith relations between Jews and Christians, and in light of the positive significance of the Torah in Judaism, the Lutheran use of "law" as God's condemning judgment that leads to death is highly problematic.[13]

Turning finally to "justification by faith," which Luther came to maintain is the key to the Scriptures, we might observe that the legal concept of justification does not appear to be an integral theme of 2 Kings 5, which is rather about the human misery caused by hostility between enemy nations and by disease. Yet, we might consider Naaman's ultimate acquiescence in following Elisha's instructions to dip in the Jordan as a kind of faith, which is followed not by a declaration of the military commander's innocence, but by his restoration to health. When Naaman then tries to compensate Elisha for curing his leprosy, he is rebuffed, since his recovery cannot be earned as in an ordinary economic transaction, but rather remains a free gift through the prophet in Samaria. Naaman has done nothing to merit or earn the healing, and he can do nothing to pay for it after the fact.

## Luther's Naaman and the Jew

It is significant that the longest interpretation of this narrative in 2 Kings 5 by Martin Luther himself, which appears in his Commentary on Galatians of 1535,[14] develops Naaman as an example of the concept of justification by faith. We will soon return to Luther's 1535 Commentary on Galatians, but before doing so we will take the occasion to provide an overview of Luther's numerous short allusions to 2 Kings 5 scattered throughout his works. For this survey, I consulted passages that mentioned 2 Kings 5 in the collected volumes of Luther's Works,[15] which I confess is not something that I normally do as a biblical scholar, even though I am Lutheran.

First of all, one must note that Luther does not write a commentary on 2 Kings. There is no sustained close reading and interpretation of the story of Naaman's conversion and healing, word by word, line by line, of the kind that we have for example in Luther's commentaries on Genesis and the Psalms, which are based on his teaching of these texts over a period of several years. Rather, allusions to verses from 2 Kings 5 appear in various other contexts, always to support some larger point that Luther is making. Certainly we don't have anything in Luther's Works like the literary analysis that I have provided, and any expectation that he might have produced this type of modern treatment would be anachronistic. Some general observations about Luther's remarks on this story are nevertheless revealing.

Perhaps the most striking thing is that Luther never mentions the little Israelite girl and her witness in his allusions to 2 Kings 5. She never captures his imagination, judging from her absence in the writings that preserve his thought. Perhaps this should come as no surprise. Living half a millennium ago, Luther did not have the benefit of several decades of feminist scholarship and of the transformation in gender roles that have revolutionized our society and our perceptions. Today new perspectives and sensibilities introduced by feminist, womanist, *mujerista*, and other voices from the margins allow us to notice and value additional dimensions of the Bible that may have been previously neglected, as well as to point out when scriptural passages are themselves limited by gender and cultural biases. Even though I am disappointed that the little Israelite girl at the center of my interpretation of 2 Kings 5:1-19 appears to have eluded Luther's attention, I am confident that, had he written a full commentary on 2 Kings, he would have made good use of this minor character and her faithful witness.[16]

By contrast, there are approximately fifty references to Naaman in Luther's writings, based on the index that I consulted. These allusions serve different purposes in different contexts. A brief overview of selected treatments of the figure of Naaman may convey the gist of Luther's understanding of this biblical figure.

Luther regards Naaman as an example of God's gift of good leaders to all nations, both within and beyond the borders of Israel.[17] As the divine king of all people, God brought deliverance and prosperity to Syria through Naaman,[18] just as God assisted Egypt through Joseph[19] and Babylon through Daniel and his companions.[20] God may spare even a wicked nation because of a single pious man such as Naaman,[21] and a dedicated government official of Naaman's caliber can lift the fortunes of an entire country.[22] Luther notes the urgent need for talented and strong leaders like Naaman in his own time,[23] and he addresses Prince Frederick, Duke of Saxony, as "another Naaman" in whom God is giving deliverance to Germany.[24] Of special interest to Luther is the honorific title, "father," with which Naaman's servants address him, indicating the respect due to office holders and other leaders.[25] Luther is highly appreciative of the role played by Naaman as the successful commander of the Aramean army, and this positive assessment is unqualified by what I perceive as the ironic perspective on this character provided by the narrative itself or by any concern about what might be considered a war crime in the capture and enslavement of a child from a defeated nation.

In Luther's writings Naaman also serves as a model of faith. His conversion through hearing the Word addressed to him by the prophet Elijah[26] was a mysterious instance of prevenient or accidental grace, outside of the covenant with Abraham with its promises of Christ.[27] As a leader of his community, Naaman responded in gratitude by establishing an ordinance leading others to the worship of God.[28] Luther expresses his own alienation with the church when he identifies with Naaman as a man who worshipped God sincerely in his heart and in the privacy of his home despite the corruption and idolatry of the local temple of Rimmon (2 Kings 5:18).[29]

Luther repeatedly emphasizes that Naaman the Syrian came to worship the true God without becoming Jewish through the observance of Mosaic law, since each nation has its own civil laws for governance.[30] According to Luther, Naaman and others in the Bible from all times and places were sanctified and became children of God without circumcision or other works of the law,[31] since they are justified by faith alone.[32]

This line of interpretation brings us back to Luther's 1535 *Commentary on Galatians*, where we find the fullest development of Namaan as an example of justification by grace without the law. Luther introduces the narrative in 2 Kings 5 in the context of his commentary on Galatians 3:2: "Did you receive the Spirit by doing the works of the law or by believing what you heard?" The pertinent passage reads:

> ... Naaman the Syrian was no doubt a good and devout man, and had a correct idea of God. And although he was a Gentile and did not belong to the kingdom of Moses, which was flourishing at that time, still his flesh was purified, the God of Israel was revealed to him, and he received the Holy Spirit. For this is what he says (2 Kings 5:17-18): "Henceforth your servant will not offer burnt offering or sacrifice to any God but the Lord. In this matter may the Lord pardon your servant: When my master goes into the house of Rimmon to worship there, leaning on my arm, when I bow myself in the house of Rimmon." And the prophet says to him (2 Kings 5:19): "Go in peace." When a Jew hears this, he goes to pieces with rage and says: "Do you mean that the Gentile is to be justified even though he has not observed the law, and that he is to be compared with us who are circumcised?"[33]

In this passage, in which Luther interprets 2 Kings 5 in the context of his *Commentary on Galatians*, we observe first of all that there is no little girl to point the way toward healing. Similarly, there are no servants to urge Naaman on to compliance when he is enraged at the prophet's simple protocol. Also absent is the bungled diplomatic mission that mocks the power of kings and military leaders and reveals the limits of war, wealth, and all that is great.

What we have instead is an improvement of Naaman's character, so that according to Luther he is "no doubt a good and devout man" with a "correct idea of God." There is no mention of Naaman's anger with the prophet, of his initial refusal to follow his instructions because of pride, and no suggestion whatsoever that he caused pain to others such as the little Israelite girl because of his success in war. Luther also enhances God's role in Naaman's conversion, when he explains that "the God of Israel was revealed to him, and he received the Holy Spirit."

Luther expresses the main point of the narrative most directly through the outraged question of an imagined Jewish commentator who suddenly appears at the conclusion of this interpretation: "Do you mean that the Gentile is to be justified even though he has not observed the law, and that he is to be compared with us who are circumcised?" For Luther, Naaman is precisely an example of justification by faith alone, without the Mosaic law and circumcision, even though as this passage earlier notes the "kingdom of Moses" (by which we might understand him to mean the independent governments of the northern and southern kingdoms of Israel and Judah) was flourishing at that time.

This interpretation stems from an astute observation that the Syrian commander was able to recognize the healing power of Israel's God and become a worshipper of this deity, even as a non-Israelite, as an outsider. We should note, however, that Luther's emphasis on justification without observance of Mosaic law and circumcision has nothing to do with 2 Kings 5 and everything to do with the larger context of the passage in Galatians on which he is commenting.

Similarly, the rage of the Jew at the end is entirely Luther's own construction. It is worth emphasizing that 2 Kings 5 is itself a "Jewish" narrative, and that the witness of a gentile to Israel's God is a frequent motif in the Hebrew scriptures. Luther may have had in the back of his mind a biblical character such as Jonah, who directed his anger at God for graciously sparing the city of Nineveh. Looking more locally at 2 Kings 5, however, it seems that Luther transferred to an imagined Jew the rage expressed in this story by Naaman, when he becomes angry at Elisha for not coming out to greet him, and for the simplicity of his requirement to dip seven times in the Jordan. Naaman becomes good, devout, and filled with the Holy Spirit, and an invented Jew assumes his rage, but at something completely different, namely at Luther's own interpretation of the story as an illustration of justification by grace through faith alone.

It is worth pausing here to ask why Luther might have invented the outraged Jew. There seem to be at least two answers to this question. We have already suggested the first, that Luther is responding to the larger contextual dynamics of his Galatians commentary. In his interpretation of 2 Kings 5 within this commentary, Luther echoes Paul's polemical tone in Galatians, in which the apostle dismisses the significance of Jewish law for gentile converts to Christianity in the first century CE, since justification is by faith in Christ Jesus alone. Luther's invention of an angry Jewish critic of his interpretation of 2 Kings 5 as an example of justification by faith apart from the works of the law appears to embody the dispute at the heart of Paul's letter to the Galatians.

But that is not the only dynamic at play. Luther's exegesis is also based on his own autobiography, including his struggles with the teachings and the leadership of the Roman Catholic Church, which he assumes to be a common experience for contemporary Christians. As Luther discloses a little further along in this same 1535 *Commentary on Galatians*, his real opponent is not the angry Jew, but the Church of his own day:

> Today we are forced to admit the same thing, since we have been convinced by the testimony of our own conscience, namely that the Spirit is not given through the law, but is given through hearing with faith. For previously, under the papacy, many have tried with great labor and effort to observe the law, the statues or decrees of the fathers, and the traditions of the pope. And some so weakened and damaged their bodies with severe and constant exercises in vigils, fasts, and prayers that finally they were not fit to do anything. Yet

all they accomplished by this performance was to torment themselves miserably. They could never arrive at the point of having a tranquil conscience and peace in Christ. On the contrary, they were perpetually in doubt concerning God's will toward them. But now, since the gospel teaches that the law and works do not justify, but that faith in Christ does, knowledge, a sure understanding, a joyful conscience, and a true judgment about every way of life and about everything else follow. Now the believer can easily judge what he could not judge before: that the papacy with all its religious orders and traditions is wicked. For such great blindness used to prevail in the world that we supposed that the works which men had invented, not only without but against the commandment of God, were much better than those which a magistrate, the head of a household, a teacher, a child, a servant, etc. did in accordance with God's command.[34]

Luther concludes this discussion with his conviction that "you cannot do anything to obtain the forgiveness of sins except only to listen to the Word of God."[35]

In this passage from his 1535 *Commentary on Galatians*, Luther highlights his own faith struggles to gain spiritual fulfillment and to earn forgiveness of sins and justification before God through conformance with all manner of church practices, decrees, and traditions. He contrasts his futile efforts with the tranquil conscience and "peace" (a key word from 2 Kings 5:19, in which Elisha sends Naaman forth in "peace") that he found through faith in Christ. Personal experience is clearly an important lens through which Luther interprets Scripture, forcefully and with creative freedom.

In light of this larger context, the imagined Jew in Luther's interpretation of 2 Kings 5 above is revealed to be a figure representing the papacy and other officials in the hierarchy of the Roman church. Luther is interpreting Scripture, including 2 Kings 5, in a polemical manner as a basis for dissent within the Christian church itself. There are, however, many other passages and even whole works in which Luther does direct scathing diatribes against the Jews, and even here the caricature of a Jew raging against grace is an example of unacceptable anti-Jewish scapegoating.

## Acknowledging Luther's Legacy

Luther's objectionable use of a raging Jew in his interpretation of 2 Kings 5 to illustrate the key concept of justification through faith calls us to acknowledge that the great reformer's legacy as a biblical interpreter is in some ways deeply problematic, especially because it is so foundational and influential. Almost five hundred years later, Lutherans of the twenty-first century can see through the vision of hindsight some of his limitations including his demonization and stereotyping of Jews and Judaism.

The fact that Luther's anti-Jewish bias and caricaturing were not atypical of the late medieval period does not make them more acceptable, and their intensity and virulence increased toward the end of his life, as evident in his recommendations in such works as "On the Jews and Their Lies." We need to be vigilant to excise and to repudiate all forms of anti-Judaism and anti-Semitism within our theological statements and within our ongoing tradition of biblical interpretation, as we have pledged to do in the 1994 *ELCA Declaration to the Jewish Community*.[36]

We can be critical of aspects of Luther's biblical interpretation and reject his anti-Jewish expressions in the strongest possible terms, and yet be faithful daughters and sons of the Lutheran Reformation. We can question Luther's uncritical admiration of Naaman the victorious military commander as a model of good government and true worship, and we can speculate that the patriarchal lenses through which he read Scripture may have obscured his vision of the little girl from Israel and her witness. Honest struggle, disagreement, repentance for the past, and bold attempts to address the current realities of our day are all part of the Lutheran legacy of biblical interpretation.

Whatever my vigorous dissent from aspects of Luther's interpretation of 2 Kings 5, I continue to admire and to be inspired by how he engaged robustly and whole-heartedly with the Bible, reading Scripture in light of his own personal faith story and in light of the important issues of his day. Luther interpreted the Bible creatively as a pastoral theologian within his own historical and religious context, with the intention of reforming the church and the world in which he found himself. This active approach to engaging Scripture as the Word of God remains central to the Lutheran legacy of biblical interpretation.

As a Lutheran biblical interpreter, I am especially appreciative of Luther's strong emphasis on education of women and lay people, largely so that they could read the Bible.[37] At least in part because of Luther's influence, "here I stand," a Lutheran, woman, lay biblical interpreter, who teaches at one of the ELCA seminaries and who continues to find comfort in and to be challenged by the encounter with the Word through the holy Scriptures.

As Lutherans, we can take Luther's example and approach Scripture as if it were addressed "to me" and to all of us, confident of the immediacy of Scripture and of its applicability to our own experiences and our own changing contexts. At the same time, we can be honest about our interpretive difficulties and even about our dissent from what we read in the Bible, when it does not appear to conform to what we know about God through our Lord Jesus Christ. We also have the freedom and the responsibility to recognize that the Scriptures are not addressed only "to me" or to our own Christian community, but that they also had other original and historical audiences through the passing centuries, and they continue to address other contemporary communities of faith not our own. All of these layers of interpretation contribute to the full meaning of Scripture as God's Word.

We can draw critically and appreciatively from earlier interpreters, including Luther, regarding the kinds of insights about God's expectations and God's grace that we will encounter through Scripture. But rather than coming to the Bible knowing beforehand precisely what it is about or mimicking previous responses or conclusions, we, like Luther, can leave ourselves open to the possibility of gaining new insight and of being transformed by being addressed by God's Word. To be a Lutheran interpreter does not mean that we need to interpret only through a select set of theological themes—not even those great themes from a proud theological heritage that will inevitably frame our reading of the Bible! We can trust Scripture to have its own integrity and witness, and to let God speak to us anew in our generation.

Recognizing Luther's faults, we will also realize that our own interpretations are flawed and partial, and that they will reveal the biases of our generation. We are grateful for God's deep mercy both on Luther's creative and bold exegesis of the Scriptures and on our own interpretive efforts.

But just as Luther urged us to "sin boldly," trusting even more boldly in God's grace, so we are called to "interpret boldly," because our God is bolder yet. The Word of God is bold, and it is gentle. It is a comfort that is deep enough for our greatest sorrows, and a challenge that will impel us forward in our vocations within the world. It is the way, the truth, and the life. It is God active in our world. It is God's good news for me and for you and for all the peoples of the world, even for the whole creation itself.

## Endnotes

[1] I would like to express my appreciation to the communities at The Lutheran Theological Seminary at Philadelphia, Lenoir-Rhyne College, and Trinity Lutheran Seminary for their robust attendance and thought-provoking reactions to successive versions of this Hein Fry Lecture during the spring semester of 2009. Insights gained in our conversations together have contributed to this final version, as well more generally to my appreciation of the dynamics of Lutheran biblical interpretation. While it would be impossible to name and thank each person to whom I am indebted individually, I need to acknowledge three people by name: David C. Ratke (Lenoir-Rhyne College) and N. Clayton Croy (Trinity Lutheran Seminary), who read formal responses to my lecture, and Robin D. Mattison (The Lutheran Theological Seminary at Philadelphia), who engaged me in extensive informal discussion concerning Lutheran hermeneutics. In addition, I would like to thank Laurie Jungling for her assistance and patience in making practical arrangements for the lecture series and in undertaking the editorial process.

The central section of this lecture consisting of the close literary reading of 2 Kings 5:1-19 is adapted from Esther M. Menn, "Child Characters in Biblical Narratives: The Young David (1 Samuel 16-17) and the Little Israelite Servant Girl (2 Kings 5:1-19)" in The Child in the Bible, ed. Marcia J. Bunge, Terence E. Fretheim, and Beverly Roberts Gaventa (Grand Rapids, Michigan: Wm. B. Eerdmans Publishing Company, 2008), 324-52. Reprinted by permission of the publisher, all rights reserved.

[2] In addition to these three traditional Lutheran ways of understanding the Word, new attention may also be given to how God is active in nature and in history, especially since nature and history are featured prominently in the Bible.

[3] Ralph Klein, "Reading the Old Testament with Martin Luther—and Without Him," Lutheran Heritage Lecture, October, 2008, Lutheran School of Theology at Chicago.

[4] Representative titles summarizing the content of 2 Kings 5 in various modern study Bibles include, "The Healing of Naaman" (Harper Collins Study Bible, Lutheran Study Bible), "The Healing of Naaman the Leper" (Jewish Study Bible), "Cure of Naaman" (Catholic Study Bible), "The Curing of the Leprosy of Naaman" (New Oxford Annotated Bible), and "Elisha Cures Naaman's Leprosy" (Oxford Study Bible). My hunch is that the parallel with the story of Jesus' healing of a leper in Mark 1:40-45, which is the Gospel reading paired with 1 Kings 5:1-14 in the

Revised Common Lectionary, may have influenced the understanding of the main point of the Old Testament narrative.

[5] I thank Edgar Krentz for pointing out this statement by Luther to me in a Faculty Colloquy, 2008, Lutheran School of Theology at Chicago. Luther, WA 10.1,1; 17.7-12 (1522), cited in Gerhard Ebeling, *Wort Gottes und Tradition: Studien zu einer Hermeneutik der Konfessionen* (Gottingen: Vanderhoeck & Ruprecht, 1964), 102. For a discussion of Luther's understanding of the relationship between the Old and New Testaments as written and spoken Word in English, see Willem Jan Kooiman, *Luther and the Bible*, trans. John Schmidt (Philadelphia: Muhlenburg Press, 1961), 200-206.

[6] Biblical quotes in the body of this essay will generally follow the NRSV, although the author may offer another translation of particular words in order to make a point apparent in the original Hebrew but not in the NRSV translation.

[7] See Cogan Mordechai and Hayim Tadmor, *The Anchor Bible*, II Kings (Garden City, New York: Doubleday, 1988), 61-67; and Jean Kyoung Kim, "Reading and Retelling Naaman's Story (2 Kings 5)," *Journal for the Study of the Old Testament* 30 (2005): 49-61.

[8] Phyllis Trible, *Texts of Terror: Literary-Feminist Readings of Biblical Narratives* (Philadelphia: Fortress Press, 1984).

[9] Elisha's name means "my God saves," which resonates with the "salvation" that the LORD gave to Aram through Naaman (2 Kings 5:1).

[10] For the Hebrew term *na'arah*, see Carolyn S. Leeb, *Away from the Father's House: The Social Location of* na'ar *and* na'arah *in Ancient Israel. Journal for the Study of the Old Testament* 30 (Sheffield: Academic Press, 2000), 301.

[11] The paraphrase "she served Naaman's wife" in the NRSV captures this sense of the word "before" (*lifne*) in the phrase "she was before (*lifne*) Naaman's wife."

[12] Nicholas Kristoff, New York Times, March 28, 2009.

[13] Esther Menn, "Law and Gospel," in conversation with Krister Stendahl, in *Covenantal Conversations: Christians in Dialogue with Jews and Judaism*, ed. Darrell Jodock, ELCA Consultative Panel on Lutheran-Jewish Relations (Minneapolis: Fortress Press, 2008), 42-60.

[14] This is Luther's second commentary on the book of Galatians, based primarily on his students' lecture notes.

[15] *Luther's Works*, 55 vols., ed. H.T. Lehman and J. Pelikan (St. Louis and Philadelphia: Fortress Press and Concordia Publishing House, 1957-1976)

[16] By contrast, Luther does notice other minor characters in 2 Kings 5 when he expresses his approval of Naaman's servants for honoring their master by addressing him respectfully as "Father." *Luther's Works* 16.180; 22.99; 51.148; cf., 25.282.

[17] *Luther's Works* 7.151; 13.155, 165, 207.

[18] *Luther's Works* 3.332; 19.84; 46.192.

[19] *Luther's Works* 13.170.

[20] *Luther's Works* 19.84.

21. *Luther's Works* 3.235; 6.217; 11.228; 16.217; cf., 46.248.
22. *Luther's Works* 7.65; 13.170; 24.80; 34.67; 46.248; cf., 13.180; 5.287.
23. *Luther's Works* 13.203.
24. *Luther's Works* 42.123.
25. *Luther's Works* 16.99, 180; 22.00; 25.282; 51.148.
26. *Luther's Works* 8.136. Luther seems to regard Naaman's dipping in the Jordan as akin to baptism in *Luther's Works* 10.283. He notes that Naaman's transport of soil from Jerusalem (sic) indicates the high regard for the Jews and their heroic kings, judges, and other wise leaders among the heathen in biblical times in *Luther's Works* 2.258.
27. *Luther's Works* 2.178; 9.302; 25.181.
28. *Luther's Works* 17.291; 47.91. In *Luther's Works* 28.364, Luther explains that the expression "Naaman the Syrian was elsewhere" indicates that there is a lack of leadership and an opportunity for false teaching.
29. *Luther's Works* 38.165; 40.95; 49.340; 52.271.
30. *Luther's Works* 14.19; 26.211; 27.287, 335; 49.74.
31. *Luther's Works* 3.81, 89; 27.335; 47.157.
32. *Luther's Works* 26.211.
33. *Luther's Works* 26.211.
34. *Luther's Works* 26.212.
35. *Luther's Works* 26.213.
36. For the full text of the 1994 *Declaration of the Evangelical Lutheran Church in America to the Jewish Community,* see www.elca.org.
37. *Luther's Works* 45.188, 370; 46.232.

# Does this Text Have a Future?
## Eschatology in Lutheran Biblical Interpretation

Mary Hinkle Shore
*Luther Seminary*

In an essay titled, "The Sermon on the Mount as Radical Pastoral Care," homiletics professor and Lutheran pastor, Richard Lischer, observes, "Contemporary Christians, however much they may admire the Sermon on the Mount, want even more to use it or to know if it is usable in the congregation."[1] A similar desire, with respect to the Bible as a whole, is behind the ELCA's Book of Faith initiative. We want the Bible to make a difference in our lives and in our life together as congregations and as a whole church. We want to know its content better, but we do not just want to know its content better. We also want our interaction with God's word to shape us into the people God intends us to be.

So, how do we get there from here? How is the Bible usable in the congregation? I am going to look with you at a couple of different understandings of what Scripture is and how it engages modern readers. I think the most promising understanding of Scripture is to see it as an (a) extended story in which we play a part, (b) with a particular main character, and (c) an ending that keeps breaking into the middle. But this is not usually the way we try to get from the Bible to daily life.

## Kernel and Husk: Finding Principles to Apply

The more common way of trying to demonstrate the Bible's relevance for our lives is to look in it for material we may apply to our lives. Take the *Life Application Study Bible*, for instance. I looked at the *Life Application Bible* both because it is such a popular edition of the Bible[2] and because its name implies the sort of thing I believe most people mean when they say they wish they knew the Bible better. An edition of Paul's letters from the Life Application editors begins with these questions:

Have you ever opened your Bible and asked the following:

- What does this passage really mean?
- How does it apply to my life?
- Why does some of the Bible seem irrelevant?
- What do these ancient cultures have to do with today?
- I love God; why can't I understand what he is saying to me through his Word?
- What's going on in the lives of these Bible people?[3]

These questions inspire casual readers as well as lifelong students of the biblical text. Answers to them vary.

Take the *Life Application Bible*'s answer, for instance. This edition of the Bible was produced to help Christians in the American evangelical tradition apply God's word to their lives, hence the name "Life Application Study Bible." The editors noticed that Christians were hearers of the Word but not doers of it. People might read the Bible—they might even understand it—but they were apparently not being changed by it. It was as if Jesus had said, "You will know the truth and then go home for Sunday dinner." The evangelical answer to this was to speak honestly about a gap between "then" and "now" and find a way to bridge the gap. The *Life Application Bible* seeks to bridge what the editors call the "timeless truth" of a biblical passage and a "personal application" to life, one person at a time.[4]

Late twentieth-century, American evangelicals were not the first to see a divide between the witness of Scripture and its modern application. Nor were they the first to attempt to bridge this perceived gap with the view of Scripture as a repository of timeless truths that could be de-contextualized and re-contextualized. Thomas Jefferson's scissors-and-paste approach to the gospels followed the same logic.[5] The most charitable construction of Jefferson's work is that he feared that the gospels, with all their wildly magical reports of miracles and wildly catastrophic reports of the end times, would be ignored by reasonable men unless someone like himself could separate the wheat from the chaff.

A bit more than a century after Jefferson, in the early 1900s, the theologian and historian, Adolf von Harnack, would write about the need to "distinguish kernel and husk" in early Christian witness. He advocated abandoning the "earliest form" of the gospel precisely to grasp and hold that "which, under differing historical forms, is of permanent validity."[6]

While I do not, finally, support the project of attempting to unbundle kernel and husk, I do sympathize with the need for some response to the fact that the better one knows the Bible, the more one feels the need to offer some explanation for it. This view—of the Bible as timeless truth mixed in with time-bound noise—almost always comes from people who want to find a way to continue to argue for Scripture's value while being honest about the human fingerprints all over the pages of God's word.

In a sermon preached to seminarians at Yale Divinity School, Leander Keck comments that the very process of Bible study itself can undermine one's sense of confidence in the Bible. "We are not sure we can use our weapons," he says. "True, we have been taught how to disassemble our rifles and to name the parts—you know, J, E, D, P, Q, Proto-Luke, and Deutero-Paul. But now we have trouble getting it back together. Some of us are afraid that when we need it most, it will not work for us the way it used to; while others wonder whether there is any firepower at all in such a scripture as the Bible turns out to be."[7]

It is not just a scholarly preoccupation. Most of us who took even one religion class in college, or who have watched Peter Jennings on Jesus, or Bill Moyers on Genesis, know the experience of wondering, at least for a while, whether anything we have been told about the Bible in church is true. What a mess of stuff is in the Bible! It's like a very old person's attic in there! How do we begin to "apply" such a mess to our lives?

One of the responses to this sort of failure of confidence in the Bible is to say that, yes, the Bible does in fact have human fingerprints all over it, but in, with, and under all that ancient worldview and patriarchal bias and ethnic chauvinism and violence is God-given truth for every age. It is a short step from this observation to the view of the Bible is a compendium of timeless truth all wrapped up in historical contingencies. The reward of careful reading, then, is that one discovers what to shuck and what to keep. Mostly, what we end up trying to glean in this view are moral principles that we can apply to our lives.

## Limitations of Kernel and Husk

For two reasons, I think this approach to interpreting the Bible is not helpful to those of us who want to live in worshipping communities shaped by Scripture. First, there is the doctrine of the Incarnation. Our God's self-revelation is routinely embedded in history and remarkably so in Jesus of Nazareth. To read that long story of God revealing God's justice, mercy, and creativity within history and conclude that the story's best contribution to our life together is as a source of illustrations from which timeless moral principles may be extracted is to fail to see that God consistently chooses to reveal God's self within time and space. Even if it could be done, why would Christians, whose most distinctive confession is the news that God was fully present in Jesus of Nazareth, seek to strip away the human, historical, incarnational elements of our sacred texts? We do not confess Jesus as an illustration of healing, or redemption, or judgment. We confess Jesus as healer, redeemer, judge. When we seek to extract principle from story, leaving plot and character behind, we are in danger of reducing Christian claims to nothing more than conventional wisdom about right and wrong.

The second reason to reject the practice of reading the Bible mainly as a sourcebook for principles to apply to our lives is that it regards the Bible as most important for what it says about us and our behavior. In fact, the Bible is more important for what it says about God. "Give God some verbs," I say to students about their sermons. The Bible gives Gods all sorts of verbs.

It is sometimes said that people go to church to be told what to do. Lutherans, I think, are more likely to go to church to find out what God has done, to hear about what God will do, and—through worship—to participate together in God's future "ahead of time." Using the Bible as a source for moral principles that we are called to live out often turns into an exercise in moralism; that is, we receive information about what we should do, but no news about how the life that is expected of us is possible or how God might be fulfilling those expectations in us (cf. Romans 8:4).

Take, for example, the note on this verse in the Life Application Study Bible: The verse is 1 Corinthians 12:26 ("And if one member suffers, all the members suffer with it; if one member is honored, all the members rejoice with it"), and the note on the verse is this:

What is your response when a fellow Christian is honored? When someone is suffering? We are called to rejoice with those who rejoice and weep with those who weep (Romans 12:15). Too often, unfortunately, we are jealous of those who rejoice and separate ourselves from those who weep. Believers are in the world together—there is no such thing as individualistic Christianity. We can't concern ourselves only with our own relationship with God, we need to get involved in the lives of others.

The note is all true. We do often ignore or resent brothers and sisters in Christ. We do focus too much on ourselves and turn Christianity into an individual pursuit. We should not do either of those things. The note is absolutely true, but it is not exactly empowering. It is as if the editors believe that all we need is information, and we will be able to do the right and avoid the wrong. Yet as anyone knows who has ever tried to introduce regular aerobic exercise or more dark leafy greens into his or her life—not to mention increasing fellow feeling for brothers and sisters in Christ—knowledge of a principle is not necessarily power to embody it.

Beyond this, the study Bible note, almost without our noticing it, has turned an indicative statement from Paul into an imperative. Paul had said, "If one member suffers, all the members suffer with it; if one member is honored, all the members rejoice with it." He is noting how bodies work. In the very next verse Paul says, "Now you are Christ's body, and individually members of it" (1 Corinthians 12:27). Paul is not exhorting the Corinthians in this verse either. He is simply reporting the news. He is updating them on their own status and making explicit the implications of that status. Suffering together, honoring one another—this is the way that members of the crucified and risen body of Christ behave, and—news flash—you people are members of that body.

If the Corinthians are not behaving in concert with what they are—and they are not, of course—Paul gives them not a list of commands, but an announcement of their true identity. In response to all the attempts of the Corinthians to rank themselves—strong vs. weak, having knowledge, not having knowledge, having spiritual gifts, having the coolest spiritual gifts—Paul offers the Corinthians an eschatological vision of the body of Christ and the relationship of its members to one another. He has given them news of their place in a story. This is who you are. This is where you are headed.

Paul does what I am proposing we do as we read the Bible together. As I said when I began, I think the most promising way of reading Scripture is to see it as an a) extended story in which we play a part, b) with a particular main character, and c) an ending that keeps breaking into the middle. Here's what I mean.

**The Bible: An extended story . . .**

The Bible is an extended story in which we play a part.

The most accessible contemporary proponent of seeing the Bible as a single long story is probably N. T. Wright. In his little book, *The Last Word: Beyond the Bible Wars to a New Understanding of the Authority of Scripture*, Wright summarizes his position like this: "The Bible itself offers a model for its own reading, which involves knowing where we are within the overall drama and what is appropriate within each act. The acts are: creation, 'fall,' Israel, Jesus, and the church; they constitute the differentiated stages in the divine drama which Scripture itself offers."[8] For Wright, the appropriate use of Scripture involves finding one's place in this story and acting in accord with that place. "We must act in the appropriate manner for this moment in the story," he writes, "this will be in direct continuity with the previous acts (we are not free to jump suddenly to another narrative, a different play altogether), but such continuity also implies discontinuity, a moment where genuinely new things can and do happen."[9] With this "five-act play" hermeneutic (creation, fall, Israel, Jesus, church), Wright hopes to find a way past what he calls, "the sterile debate between people who say, 'The Bible says . . .' and those who answer, 'Yes, and the Bible also says you should stone adulterers, and you shouldn't wear clothes made of two types of cloth.'"[10]

Whether or not Wright's proposal will get us where we need to go, he is certainly correct that we need a way beyond that stalemate. He is also correct that when we read the Bible, we are reading the long story of God's interaction with humanity, a story that continues into our own time and includes us.

**. . . with a particular main character . . .**

This story, of which we are a part, has one particular main character—God who, when we get to the New Testament, is made manifest in the person of Jesus. I mention this to oppose versions of narrative theology or narrative appreciation that just seem to like a good story. I am speaking against the view that plot is more important than character. In his homiletics text, *Preaching Jesus,* Charles Campbell tells the story of a student summarizing the children's book, *Are You My Mother?* in a paper and concluding with this comment: "The young bird is lost and alone. He thinks a bulldozer is his mother. His real mother saves him from being hurt and brings him home. The gospel is told."[11]

This student's mistake is one that seasoned preachers make as well. Loving stories, we can end up favoring plot over character. The children's story is not unlike the big story of Scripture: it is a story of a relationship lost and restored; it is a story of danger, foolishness, and rescue, a story where things work out in the end. Yet it is not therefore accurate to conclude upon telling it that "the gospel is told." As Campbell concludes, "It is not narrative form that is key to Scripture. Rather . . . it is the One whose identity is rendered by the narratives in the Bible who is the key. 'Story' cannot save or empower us. Rather, it is God in Jesus Christ, whom the biblical narratives identify, who saves and empowers."[12] It is a completely obvious point that we routinely miss when reading Scripture. This stuff is about God and about God's son, Jesus.[13]

### . . . and an ending that keeps breaking into the middle.

It makes sense, then, in an attempt to recognize how the Bible is relevant to our lives, to ask what the Bible's main character is up to. Since I teach New Testament, I am going to focus here on New Testament texts. The claim throughout the New Testament, however, is that the central task of Jesus is announcing and embodying the kingdom of God at hand, and that the God whose reign Jesus announces and embodies is none other than the God revealed in Israel's scriptures.

Jesus comes proclaiming the kingdom of God, and as a result of his words and actions, the kingdom of God is, indeed, manifest. The end breaks into the middle of the story. There are other more vivid ways of saying the same thing. In his essay titled, "The Limits of Story," Richard Lischer has remarked, "Eschatology reminds us that faith is a slash across the symmetry or predictability of history."[14] Carl Braaten has argued, "The end of history has appeared in Jesus of Nazareth without ceasing to be future."[15] Braaten also remarks that Jesus "made present the reality of God's future in a concentrated way."[16]

It is, by the way, this non-linear reality of the biblical story that leads to my dissatisfaction with N. T. Wright's proposal that we read the Bible differently depending on where in a linear drama we are located. Offering an analogy to explain his position, Wright says, "If someone in the fifth act of *All's Well That Ends Well* were to start repeating speeches from earlier acts, instead of those which belonged to the fifth act itself, the whole play would begin to unravel."[17] Well, I am not so sure. In fact, I am arguing that this kind of repeating of speeches from earlier acts, as well as announcements from a future last act that Wright does not include among the five he names, is precisely what is happening in the Bible and what should happen in our use of the Bible.

## The First Words of Jesus in the Gospels

Look, for example, at the first words of Jesus in each of the gospels. Each scene directs the reader's eye toward something associated with Israel's hopes, and each scene points to those hopes being fulfilled in the present time. In Matthew the first thing Jesus does is to talk John into baptizing him "in order to fulfill all righteousness." In the same gospel Jesus will say he has come, not to abolish the law, but to fulfill it. A righteous people of God was the dream and the call of the Israel's prophets. Jesus embodies that dream even as he teaches, feeds people, and heals diseases.

In Mark, Jesus first says, "The kingdom of God is at hand; repent, and believe the good news!" From the first of Israel's kings through to the Roman Caesars and their local puppet rulers, a human king had been a concession on God's part and a mixed blessing for the people. To announce God's kingdom was to proclaim limits on the power of existing human rulers and to look toward Israel and God being restored to one another.

In Luke, Jesus first speaks at age twelve, and then it is to say, "Did you not know that I would be in my Father's house?" As exasperating as the comment must be to his mother, Jesus calls to mind the vision of Isaiah that the temple will someday be a place for everyone to learn the requirements of God (cf. Isaiah 2:1-4). It will be the place to look not only for the people of Israel but also for the nations.

In John's gospel, Jesus speaks first by asking two of John's disciples what they are looking for as they follow him. When they reply by asking,

"Where are you staying?" Jesus says, "Come and see." Just about the first thing they see, of course, is Jesus, in spite of the fact that his "hour has not yet come" (John 2:4), changing water into wine. The eschatological banquet begins—ahead of time, perhaps—as the steward congratulates the bridegroom on having saved the best wine for last.

Do you see what I mean about the end breaking into the middle? As it is for kids on a road trip, the answer for us, too, is "No, we're not there yet." Nonetheless, it is also true that "there" keeps appearing "here" at odd times.

## The Raising of Lazarus

The texts where the end most explicitly gets mixed up with the middle are the Bible's resurrection stories. After Lazarus dies, for example, Jesus says to Martha, "Your brother will rise again" (John 11:23). Martha apparently understands Jesus to be saying something like, "You know, Martha, it will all work out in the end," because she replies, "I know that he will rise again in the resurrection on the last day." But Martha has not understood Jesus, and so he replies, "I am the resurrection and the life." Jesus is not talking only about the last day. He is talking about this day. Jesus is about to pull the future right into the present. "I am the resurrection and the life"—present tense, now.

Of course, it is better not to make a promise like that unless you can keep it. Standing there, outside the tomb, hollering at a man whose ears are probably already jelly, Jesus keeps his word. Lying there inside the tomb for four days, yet still at some great distance from the last day, Lazarus hears Jesus and rises. Lazarus walks out of the tomb, and, in that moment, the future and the present cannot be so neatly distinguished from each other as they could before.

All this, as you know, gets Jesus into trouble. This confusion of present and future, and the stir of faith it causes, are disturbing to some people whose biggest dream is for the present to stretch out in time as far as the eye can see. These people apply themselves to the task of making Jesus history. For a couple of days, it looks like they have managed it. They would manage it altogether, except that the Father will not leave the Son without a present and a future.

That second resurrection in the gospel of John confirms that in the first one, when Jesus raises Lazarus, it is more than a personal favor to his personal friends. When he yells at Lazarus to come out of the tomb alive, Jesus is making the glory of God known. Outside that tomb, with his word bringing the future right into the present, the Son is doing the Father's work. The Father does the same work himself when he raises Jesus from the dead.

## The Impact of a Trusted Promise on Christian Life

At this point, you may be wondering whether I have forgotten that my original question was how to use the Bible in Christian life and in Christian communities. I began by suggesting Christians generally want the Bible to make a difference in our lives and in our life together as congregations and as a whole church. I rejected attempts to make the Bible relevant to personal or corporate life by reducing its content to so-called timeless principles or moral imperatives for application to one's life, and I proposed instead that it was both more accurate and more practical to see the Bible as an extended story, with a particular main character and an ending that keeps breaking into the middle.

So what about that "practical" part? How does this way of looking at the Bible work? How does it change the way we read Scripture and the way we put Scripture into practice in our lives? To answer those questions, I want to introduce the category of promise. Describing the character and function of a promise, Richard Lischer writes,

> The promise reveals commitment, reliability, and even passion in the one who promises. It is not merely a message. A message can be detached from its point of origin or from its sender. A promise cannot. A promise loses its very character apart from the one who promises. If I am out of work and on relief, and the owner of the local grocery store promises me a job in two weeks, whether or not I now adopt a stance of hope in the world depends on the character of the one who promises. Does he have a history of faithful actions from which I can abstract the quality of faithfulness and ascribe it to him? Are there testimonies to his faithfulness? If so, my life has already changed. It changes with the issuance of the promise.[18]

To say that the end of the biblical story breaks into the middle is to say that the main character of the story demonstrates the capacity and the will to make good on the story's promises even before the story is over, and such trust-inspiring behavior creates faith in those with whom it is shared.

When Paul talks about the Holy Spirit given as a "first installment" or "guarantee"[19] of redemption, he is identifying for his readers just such an "ahead of time," faith-creating experience. Paul's language describes the current reality of those to whom God has given the Holy Spirit using this imagery: We have received earnest money from one who is good for the rest of the payout. We live in the time after which a promise has been issued and before it is fulfilled. It is like having the promise of a job. You have not started working yet, but you get up in the morning and do not read the classifieds first. You are thinking ahead to your first day on the job. You buy a lunch bag. Your life has already changed.

## Hermeneutics: Reading Scripture As a Promise

In the actual picking up of the Bible and reading, then, my understanding of Scripture suggests some questions to put to the text. Instead of asking, "How do I apply this text to my life?" I suggest we ask questions like these: 1) "What just happened?" 2) "What does the future look like?" and 3) "What now?"

### What just happened?

Focal text: Matthew 18:25-35

First, say what you see. What just happened? Putting this question to a biblical text before other questions slows us down enough that we notice who is acting in a text, who is speaking, what is happening with respect to time, and what is happening to the characters. When New Testament stories take a tragic turn, the tragedy is often tied to the characters' failure to realize that something very big has happened. Take, for example, the story Jesus tells Peter when Jesus is explaining forgiveness and the kingdom of heaven. The text is Matthew 18:23-35. Peter and Jesus have just had a conversation about how many times one might be expected to forgive the same member of the community. Peter suggests seven. Jesus suggests more: seventy seven times, he says. An answer like that makes it sound as if Jesus expects repentance and forgiveness to be one of the rhythms of life in community instead of a commodity to be measured out more or less generously.

Then Jesus tells the story of the unforgiving servant. Here we have a guy who actually lives in a world characterized by forgiveness. The tragedy, both for himself and his neighbor, is that nothing about his behavior gives evidence that he knows it. He cannot pay—will probably never be able to pay—the debt he owes, and in response to his plea for mercy, his master forgives his debt. It is like the year of Jubilee or something. The slate is wiped clean. The kingdom is at hand, and it's good news! He is forgiven an astronomical debt—and he acts as if nothing at all has changed. He walks away from having a huge debt forgiven as if nothing had happened. Could that happen to us? Could we receive what amounts to a whole new life and miss it?

The question also provides a way to reflect on the present reaction to the reading of the text: What just happened? Most of us know the experience of reading a text like the parable of the unforgiving servant in worship. We finish the reading, look out at the people, and say, "The gospel of the Lord." The people respond, "Thanks be to God," and then a nervous laugh ripples through the crowd. What just happened there, in the community at worship? The same questions we pose to the text also work as a way for us to reflect on our own experience of having heard the Word. How is the story inspiring fear or trust? How is it attracting or repelling us? Where would we argue with it, and on what basis?[20] Each person's answers offer a window on how this particular Word has "cut a slash across the symmetry or predictability"[21] of our own history.

**What does the future look like?**

Based on the text we are reading, what can we imagine about the future? Based on this text, what, if anything, about our current experience looks like the future being pulled into the present? How is the end of the story breaking into the middle?

In the story of the unforgiving servant, the slave walks out of the meeting where Jubilee has been enacted, after which the appropriate response is to say is something like, "Bartender, drinks for everyone!" and instead, he pounces on a fellow slave who owes him what amounts to a few months wages and shakes him down for the money. When the man begs for mercy, just as he himself had begged moments before, the first slave shows no mercy. None. Technically, of course, he is within his rights to ask for what is owed him. That is a perfectly natural way of understanding how the present will plod forward into the future. The ink in the ledger never fades. It is the way the world works, right?

But what makes this parable so arresting is that is not the way the world is working here. Here, someone just tore a page right out of the ledger, and the forgiven debtor sees nothing of the implications of that missing page. Instead of recognizing his future in the world just ushered in by the master's mercy, he goes right on living in the world of red ink. The tragedy (and the justice?) of the parable is that, in the last scene of the parable, the world that the slave has acted as if he were living in becomes, in fact, his real world. What the future looks like now, at the end of the story, is one day after another imprisoned and tortured. Welcome to the rest of your life, Mr. Debtor.

In the parable, hyperbole abounds in order that the contrast between the slave's two alternative futures may be drawn as dramatically as possible: The first slave's debt is huge, and the master is all-merciful to him. Then the slave is over-the-top mean to one who owes a pittance in comparison to his forgiven debt. In response, the judgment is swift; the punishment is unprecedented in its harshness (this is the only place in the New Testament where "torturers" are mentioned), and the sentence is interminable if the man is truly to be imprisoned until he could pay the debt.

And none of it had to happen. A completely new world was opened up for the slave, and he just kept living in the old one. If Paul were telling this parable, I imagine that at the end of it he would jump up and down and wave his arms, echoing Isaiah, "See, now is the acceptable time; see, now is the day of salvation!" (2 Corinthians 6:2; cf. Isaiah 49:8).

**Given that future, what now?**

Given that the acceptable time just arrived, what now? If we were not there already, the third question we put to biblical texts ushers us into the realm of Christian ethics. If Scripture is an eschatological Word from God offering forgiveness of sins, life, and salvation ahead of the last judgment, what now? Given that all your debts are paid, what now? Is it "Drinks for everyone!" or business as usual? When you are out of work and on relief, and the owner of the local grocery store offers you a job in two weeks, has your life changed or not?

Jürgen Moltmann says that a promise "always creates an interval of tension between the uttering and the redeeming of the promise. In so doing it provides man with a peculiar area of freedom to obey or disobey, to be hopeful or resigned."[22] The level of discomfort generated by this "interval of tension," this "peculiar area of freedom," may be one of the reasons that methods of Bible study that leave us, not so much with an open future as with a moral principle to apply to our lives, are so popular. There is a persistent temptation to believe that we would behave better if we were just told what better was. Interestingly, however, the master in the parable says nothing at all to the formerly indebted servant about what to do if he should meet up with someone who owes him a little money. Would the story have worked out better if the master had so instructed the slave?

I do not know. But I do know that it would have been a different story. If the master had made a deal with the slave—"I'm going to forgive your debt, and you should pay it forward"—it would not have been a story about a new, wide-open, debt-free future. It would have been a story about a bargain struck between a master and his servant: "I'll do this, and then you will do that." The servant would not have been free of obligation. He would have just traded a large obligation for a small one. Then, if he did not forgive the tiny debt of his fellow slave, we could all look on and say, "What a loser. He didn't hold up his end of the bargain." But the master is not making a bargain. He is making a whole new world. The man is not a loser as much as a fool for going on as if nothing had changed.

So, the question is, "What now?" and the answer is something like, "Wow, would you take a look at this place! A minute ago I was on the verge of being held without bond, and now I am walking out into the sunshine!" Just noticing the end breaking into the middle goes a long way toward figuring out what to do next. After Lazarus is raised from the dead, Jesus wipes away his tears and says, "Unbind him and let him go." The next time we see Mary, Martha, and Lazarus, they are celebrating with dinner for everyone and with a very expensive anointing for Jesus (cf. John 12:1-8).

That anointing helps clarify what it means—and does not mean—to notice that the end appears in the middle of the story. Because the central character of our story is the Holy Trinity, one God, and because the central news of our story is the faithfulness of the Son to the Father, even to death on a cross, as well as the faithfulness of the Father to the Son, even to raising him from the dead, noticing does not mean just looking for glimpses of a future when everything has worked out nicely. Mary, Martha, Lazarus, and Jesus rejoice that Lazarus is alive. Mary anoints Jesus with pure nard so that the house is "filled with the fragrance of the perfume" (John 12:4). Jesus also sees in that event not only celebration but also the part of the future that includes his death, and when Judas complains about the waste, Jesus replies, "Leave her alone. She bought it so that she might keep it for the day of my burial" (John 12:7). Noticing the future breaking into the present is not the same as looking on the bright side or hoping for the best.

Jürgen Moltmann speaks to this issue in an essay reflecting on the events of September 11, 2001. In "Watching for God," Moltmann commends an "open-eyed mysticism" that is as much watching as it is praying and that constitutes "the wakeful expectation of God."[23] He explains: "To go through life with eyes open for God, to see Christ in oppressed and unimportant people—that is what praying and watching is all about. We believe so that we can see, not so that we can shut our eyes to the world. We believe so that we can see—and can endure what we see."[24] Moltmann chooses his words—watch and pray—of course, from the passion narrative, and he observes, "Concentration; praying; waking up; watching and praying: all this reveals to our lives the daybreak colors of the future, and it leads to the call of Jesus, who, having watched and prayed in Gethsemane, called to his sleeping disciples: 'Get up, let us be going.'"[25] This is another place where the strict linearity of some views of biblical narrative fail to describe our experience accurately. Resurrection and cross are both past events and also both in our present and our future.

## Conclusion

Christians want the Bible to make a difference in our lives and in our common life as the church. Too often readers of the Bible have seen its contribution to our life in terms of rules, some of which must either be adapted for a new time, others of which are not subject to change. Ethical arguments among Christians who understand the Bible in this way often center on which rules are to be maintained as written and which may be seen as context-bound and therefore not binding for the present time.

I am proposing a different way. Rather than looking to the Bible as a more or less accessible collection of rules for daily living, I propose that the Scriptures direct our daily lives by shaping a moral imagination: They place us in God's story and reveal to us where that story is headed. Through them, God gives us "a future and a hope" (Jeremiah 29:11 RSV). That future and hope provide the context for the decisions and actions required by our daily lives and our life together in Christian community.

## Endnotes

1. Richard A. Lischer, "The Sermon on the Mount as Radical Pastoral Care," *Interpretation* 41 (1987): 157.
2. Its publisher claims that it is "Today's #1 selling study Bible" (Tyndale House web page, http://www.tyndale.com/products/biblesref/, accessed 2/7/09).
3. *Living Letters from the Life Application™ Bible* (Wheaton, Illinois: Tyndale House, 1986), 5. For more on the motivation behind the development of the Life Application Bible, see "Why the Life Application Study Bible is Unique," http://www.lifeapplicationbible.com/what.htm#what, accessed 2/5/09.
4. *Ibid.* This answer is not so different from the distinction that the Lutheran, Krister Stendahl, proposed between what the text meant and what it means. See his "Biblical Theology, Contemporary," *Interpreters Dictionary of the Bible* (Nashville: Abingdon, 1962) 1:418-32.
5. Thomas Jefferson, *The Jefferson Bible: The Life and Morals of Jesus of Nazareth* (Boston: Beacon Press, 1989).
6. Adolf Von Harnack, *What Is Christianity?* trans. Thomas Bailey Saunders, (Philadelphia: Fortress Press, 1986), 13ff.
7. Leander E. Keck, "Limited Resources, Unlimited Possibilities," in Eugene L. Lowry, *How To Preach a Parable* (Nashville: Abingdon, 1989), 80ff.
8. N. T. Wright, *The Last Word: Beyond the Bible Wars to a New Understanding of the Authority of Scripture* (New York: HarperCollins, 2005), 121.
9. *Ibid.*, 123.
10. *Ibid.*, 121.
11. Charles L. Campbell, *Preaching Jesus: New Directions for Homiletics in Hans Frei's Postliberal Theology* (Grand Rapids, Michigan: Wm. B. Eerdmans Publishing Company, 1997), 170.
12. *Ibid.*, 172.
13. At the risk of belaboring an obvious point, I offer one more bit of data related to it. Richard Burridge, *What are the Gospels? A Comparison with Graeco-Roman Biography*, SNTS Monograph Series 70 (Cambridge: Cambridge University Press, 1992), documents the results of having run several linguistic analyses of a collection of Greco-Roman biographies and the same analyses on the four canonical gospels. Burridge discovered that the gospels have various things in common with

Greco-Roman biographies, including the fact that a single character is the subject of many of the verbs. Burridge observed about the gospel of Mark, "Jesus himself is the subject of about a quarter of the verbs (24.4 %) and a further fifth occur on his lips, in his teaching or parables (20.2%)." Burridge adds, "[N]o other individual scores above 1%" (196). The numbers are similar in Matthew and Luke and even higher in the gospel of John. No one else gets anywhere near the same number of verbs. The gospels, it turns out, are overwhelmingly focused on Jesus.

[14] Richard A. Lischer, "The Limits of Story," *Interpretation* 38 (1984) : 26-38.

[15] Carl E. Braaten, *The Future of God* (New York: Harper & Row, 1969), 25. For having pointed me in the direction of this and other sources, I am grateful to F. LeRon Shults, "The Futurity of God in Lutheran Theology," *Dialog* 42/1 (2003): 42.

[16] Carl E. Braaten, "The Recovery of Apocalyptic Imagination," in *The Last Things: Biblical and Theological Perspectives on Eschatology*, ed. Carl E. Braaten and Robert W. Jenson (Grand Rapids, Michigan: Wm. B. Eerdmans Publishing Company, 2002), 20.

[17] Wright, *The Last Word*, 122ff.

[18] Richard A. Lischer, "Preaching and the Rhetoric of Promise," *Word & World* 8 (1988): 73.

[19] The Greek word αρραβών (*arrabôn*) occurs at 2 Corinthians 1:22 and 5:5, and at Ephesians 1:14. About the word, *A Greek-English Lexicon of the New Testament and Other Early Christian Literature*, 3rd ed., ed. Danker, et al. (Chicago: University of Chicago Press, 2000) notes that in commerce the word refers to a payment "which secures a legal claim to the article in question, or makes a contract valid" and one "that obligates the contracting party to make further payments."

[20] Reflecting on this kind of the interaction with the Bible, Barbara Brown Taylor writes, "My relationship with the Bible is not a romance but a marriage, and one I am willing to work on in all the usual ways: by living with the text day in and day out, by listening to it and talking back to it, by making sure I know what is behind the words it speaks to me and being certain I have heard it properly, by refusing to distance myself from the parts of it I don't like or understand, by letting my love for it show up in the everyday acts of my life" (*The Preaching Life* [Cambridge: Cowley Publications, 1993], 56).

[21] See. note 12, above.

[22] Jürgen Moltmann, *Theology of Hope* (New York: Harper & Row, 1967), 104.

[23] Jürgen Moltmann, "Watching for God," in *Walking with God in a Fragile World*, ed. James Langford and Leroy S. Rouner (Lanham, Maryland: Rowman & Littlefield, 2003), 66.

[24] *Ibid.*, 70.

[25] *Ibid.*, 67.

# Sensus Literalis
## Another View on Luther's Legacy and Modern Readers of the Bible

Steed Vernyl Davidson
*Pacific Lutheran Thological Seminary*

When the Creation Museum opened seven miles west of the Cincinnati Airport in May 2007, most Lutherans might have missed the pride of place given to Martin Luther in this 70,000 foot theological exhibit. Luther stands as the only highly regarded non-biblical person in the entire museum. His bold stance against the excesses of a church alienated from the Bible, his position against scientists like Copernicus, his clear articulation on the age of the earth and its support in the biblical text, as well as his defense of the Bible in general, make him an important hero for persons who would otherwise not find common ground with many contemporary Lutherans. That Young Earth Creationists find Luther's words, witness, and writings appealing for their reading of Genesis, and that members of the ELCA and kindred bodies at best restrict Luther to a product of his proto-scientific age, reflect more on how far the ELCA has moved from Luther than on Luther himself. This homage to Luther in the Creation Museum conscripts him as the progenitor of a literal reading of the Bible.

In an article dated February 1984 and published on the website of the organization Answers in Genesis (the parent company of the Creation Museum), Paul Bartz pronounces that Luther regularly cites the creation narratives in Genesis as evidence of the clarity of Scripture. He drafts Luther's words and writings to his cause by making him reject outright the allegorical method in preference for a "literal" reading of the text.

He also skillfully presents Luther as a biblical scholar who understands the misordering of the creation of light before the sun, the main source of light, in the text but chastises those who make much of this as the purveyors of misleading allegories. Bartz's work liberally quotes *Luther's Works* and several of the best translations of *Luther's Works*. Yet Bartz not only holds to his version of the creation, but also re-creates Luther into the champion of his *cause célèbre*.[1]

Luther's heritage among Protestants of all varieties, and increasingly "new evangelicals"[2] dotted along the theological spectrum, stands as the centrality and uniqueness of the Bible summed up as *sola scriptura*. Simplistically, many persons view the Reformation as giving the Bible back to the world and bringing the world back to the Bible. They see Luther and the Reformers as ordering life after the Bible in a way that makes the Bible provide answers to the complexities of life, whether national, deeply personal, or merely personal. A number of Sunday school jingles like the following capture this position:

> The B-I-B-L-E.
> That's the book for me.
> I stand alone on the Word of God.
> The B-I-B-L-E.

Or perhaps you have sung or heard sung, this one:

> When there's no good in your good mornings,
> too much hell in your hello,
> And your kind heart is something less than kind;
> When you're thinking more about the thorns
> than you are the rose,
> Jesus is the answer every time.
> Use the Bible for a rule book, and I think you're gonna find
> Jesus is the answer every time[3]

These represent not merely the Reformation ideal of using Scripture as the touchstone for theological formulation, but they elevate Scripture as the touchstone for life's minutest details. This position represents the collapsing, to the point of elimination, of the distance between the world of the Bible and the contemporary world, rather than an articulated understanding of the function of the ancient text in a new generation. According to this view, the ability of the Bible to speak with such nearness to the previously unknown and lived experiences of today occurs primarily because the words of the text apply similarly today as they operated before.

While a number of steps lie between Martin Luther and the purveyors of this argument, Luther's signal work in relation to the Reformation and the usage and popularization of terms *sola scriptura* and "literal sense" make him the go-to person for those who wish to find an ancient sympathetic figure to undergird their cause. The contemporary notions of literal readings of the Bible evolve over time. The innovative work of the Jewish commentator Rashi[4] and Luther's subsequent emphasis on the plain sense of the text help set the stage for current understandings of the literal. The historical-critical method,[5] with its relentless work on the history behind the text and its recovery in some instances of a live history that gives life to the words of the Bible, also aids in developing the notion that the literal words point to an actual history that holds the same meaning today as it did in the past.

In the search to encounter what the Bible means for their times, readers of every age define a hermeneutical vision that consists of reified, abstract concepts that serve to incarnate the details of the Bible in their lives. Luther's notion of the literal sense performs this function by taking an abstraction and concretizing it as the basis for interpretation—by the search for verifiable realities in the Bible by taking the abstractions of recreated, and at times, fictive histories as the ground for asserting the complete validity of every word of the Bible. While the modern literalists may share the same philosophical ground with Luther, that may be all they hold in common. Obviously, the notion of literal[6] readings of the Bible, popular in today's religious settings, misreads and misrepresents Luther's position on Scripture. In order to show the differences and capture Luther's articulation of the literal approach to the Scripture, it will be necessary to situate Luther within the context of patristic and medieval biblical discourses. This serves as the first task of this essay.

The second task of this essay connects Luther's positions with that of the contemporary literalists and their desire for accessibility to the biblical texts. Ultimately, this essay explores the question of how to enable engagement of the Bible in contemporary faith settings and how Luther's legacy of *sensus literalis* achieves this.

The method of reading the Bible that Martin Luther pursued represents continuity with approaches already taken as well as discontinuity. As an Augustinian monk, he learned the fourfold *quadriga* of reading the Scripture at multiple levels and deriving multiple meanings. This medieval practice builds upon centuries of philosophical and theological thinking that grows out of the dominant cultural norms of the patristic periods. This fourfold method regards all scriptural texts as having at least four levels of meaning. The first level consists of the allegorical meaning and holds that elements of the text point to a mystery beyond and greater than themselves. This essentially results in concrete elements in a texts becoming spiritual realities. The second aspect of the *quadriga* lies in the anagogical sense of the text that takes the spiritual meaning from the allegorical sense to reveal a greater heavenly secret. The tropological sense represents the third aspect of the method and provides the moral guidance needed to lead a good life and to enhance the practice of withdrawal. These three senses can be regarded as the spiritual sense of the Scriptures and mark the dominant approach to reading for quite some time. The fourth aspect lies in the historical sense of the text and stands as the most variable aspect of this methodological approach.[7]

The Bible inherently offers no self-identification that suggests how it should be read.[8] In some ways, the New Testament writings participate in the philosophical, interpretive world of Greco-Roman society inasmuch as they share the literary character of that world. To this extent, they suggest the reading approaches to the entire Bible insofar as they are thought of being intentionally written to form part of a collected work known as the "Bible." Consequently, specific conventions develop over time and become normative for the church's notion of the text as sacred Scripture. Supremely, the understanding of Scripture as a text to be read grows out of the general Platonic and Aristotelian thought and the wider conventions of the Greco-Roman world. These philosophical schools influence the church fathers and later medieval thinkers and shape their hermeneutical predisposition. The *quadriga*,[9] in many ways, represents a culturally cued reading of the Bible that grows into a universally accepted approach. To the extent that a "grammar of Scripture" exists, it is a grammar of the rhetorical and interpretive forms of the Greco-Roman world.

Plato's world of forms in which things that exist point to a higher, purer form influences the art of hermeneutics and exegesis in the patristic period. Interpreters learn that even words of text point to a higher reality and, as Manfred Oeming puts it, the "good exegete must free herself from such lowly errors and ascend to the true spiritual meaning of the work."[10] In the first century C.E., among Jews and Christians, the spiritual meaning of texts offered the true message for Scripture. The work of Philo of Alexandria provides an example of allegorical readings of Hebrew texts much in line with how Christian thinkers like Origen would approach these texts, except with the christological overlay.[11] Platonic dualism feeds the christological approach to the Old Testament and at the same time affirms the validity of the New Testament. The deeper meaning of the New Testament texts can only be derived if one begins with the lower forms in the Old Testament texts.[12] The Old Testament texts represent the tactile world, in Platonic terms, while the New Testament with its concern for Jesus Christ marks the full spiritual reality. The movement from external reality to spiritual reality, from outer to inner, from lower to higher, takes place between these two divisions of the Bible but also helps construct the overarching view of how these texts should be read.

Origen marks a high point in the use of these "spiritual" approaches to reading Scripture. In Origen, the convergence of method and reader as essential to the production of the desired meaning embedded within the pages of Scripture occurs. Origen's embrace of the allegorical method grows out of his Platonic thinking. He sets up a hierarchy of meaning within texts in the same way that he views divisions within human nature. Therefore, the tripartite construction of humanity into body, soul, and spirit, where the spirit stands as the highest order, equates with the physical text and the reading process. In this system, allegory is the highest point of meaning in a text apprehended only by those with the appropriate spiritual condition to engage at this level.[13] Essentially, the reading of Scripture through the allegorical method becomes a spiritual practice and takes place largely within monasteries and priestly orders. As a method, the *quadriga* serves only a small and closed population intent on advancing their spiritual experiences, not a general Bible reading public.

The other philosophical impact on reading practices in the patristic period comes from Aristotle. The standard distinction between Plato and Aristotle—of Plato being otherworldly and Aristotle being this worldly—applies here. For as much as Platonic forms enable readers to look at words and garner a deeper spiritual meaning on a higher level, particulars as the basis for the formation of knowledge avoid seeing words as stumbling blocks to meaning, but rather as signifying something that can be known. For Platonists, words are mere shadows of a larger reality that exists beyond the words themselves. Readers need to get beyond the words to that reality. In Aristotelian thought words perform the work of signs by pointing to a thing. This enables closer scrutiny of texts themselves and develops into interest in language, words, and signs ultimately forming the basis for the practice of exegesis. Aristotle's other major contribution comes from his conception of causality as the basis for all reality.[14] If the Scriptures' first cause is God as its author, then the intentions of that author explain the reality that it caused. Reading of the biblical texts, therefore, requires probing God's intention as the basis for establishing the meaning of Scripture. The inspiration of Aristotle results in two major developments in the reading of texts—the attention to words that will evolve into the technical practice of philology and the conception that authorial intention determines the meaning of texts.

These two philosophical schools converge and at times diverge to shape the direction of biblical hermeneutics throughout much of history. Oeming, though, prefers to see it as more of a history of struggle between these two major philosophical viewpoints—"between speculative striving for the otherworldly and sober analysis of this world itself, between poetic conversation and cool, formal logic."[15] Nonetheless, the impact of Greco-Roman philosophical thought upon the reading of the Bible remains clear.

The philosophical underpinnings of biblical hermeneutics may take their starting points from Greco-Roman thought, but they reflect a decided Christian practice, articulated by major Christian figures. While Augustine receives credit as a shaper of Christian reading practices, a number of commitments already existed by the time of Augustine. Even Augustine himself needs orientation into established Christian practices, coming as he did with a plethora of influences. His Manichean tendencies initially lead him to reject the materialist nature of the text, especially the Old Testament, until schooled in allegory by Ambrose.[16] Augustine views the written text and its actual words as the gateway to a larger spiritual reality. He accepts that at times the text may be obscure and hinder progress of the spiritual meaning. However, he sees this as the opportunity to discover deeper gifts of God in the text and to keep humans humble.[17] Augustine therefore separates the literal from the spiritual in his reading practice. His reading practice, though, consists of the search for the essential virtues of faith, hope, and love, and in keeping with 1 Corinthians 13, "the greatest of these is love."[18] This hermeneutical principle that regards the Scripture as supremely communicating love informs the way Augustine distinguishes between the literal and the spiritual. The text plainly teaches love in its literal character and requires no further inquiry in which case Augustine regards the spiritual meaning as already being communicated through the literal sense. However, when obscure texts mask the virtues, the other spiritual senses help make the meaning clear.[19] Augustine holds to these distinct levels of meaning in a text that at times are clear and easy to understand and at other times obscure. A literal meaning of the texts teaches the concept of love in unambiguous ways in which case the literal serves as the vehicle for the spiritual level of meaning. More obscure texts require getting past the literal to the spiritual senses.

To read Augustine and the early reading practitioners as holding for one essential meaning that comes through the Bible in various ways distorts their position. From as early as Origen, the notion of God as the author of the Scriptures conveys the idea of a mysterious text,[20] highly complex and unlike any document written by humans. Therefore, they believe that God invests the text with mystery by suspending from the human authors meaning that will only become evident to later readers. They also believe that God complexifies the material, that it requires multiple approaches and holds meanings on several levels. Therefore, a reading of Scripture consists of a spiritual experience to understand the mind of God contained in the texts. The literal and spiritual do not stand as entities opposite each other but form part of a whole reality, albeit the literal sense cannot communicate the fullness of God. These commitments remain normative in the Church up until the medieval period, and they define the dominant approach to the Scripture as allegory. William Yarchin offers that, given the view of the mysterious nature of the sacred texts, allegory surfaced as the preferred method since it convinced the users that they were participating in the mysteries of God.[21]

By the medieval period, even though most of the norms set out from the time of Augustine remain in use, the relation of the literal sense to the other spiritual senses comes up for debate. The debate lies not in an adversarial stance that pits the literal against the spiritual, although at times the rhetoric in some parts sounds antagonistic,[22] but rather in how much importance the literal sense holds in relation to the spiritual senses and the extent to which this helps to apprehend these. From the patristic period onward, the literal sense equals the historical, but during the medieval period the relationship slowly drifts apart with a separation between what words convey and what history purports. Hugh of St. Victor, a champion for the literal sense,[23] expresses concern for both words and history. His insistence on the literal lies in the fact that interpretation can only take place through reading the "letter" since words signify words and other things. Meaning can only be constructed through words as its starting point, Hugh contends. His reading of the Old Testament forms the basis of his understanding of the literal sense of the text. He locates the literal sense of the text in the history and words of the Old Testament. However, the literal sense that would admit to a spiritual meaning exists in abeyance awaiting the "occurrence of New Testament events before they can be understood properly."[24] Although Hugh demonstrates interest in history as a formative notion of the literal sense of the Scriptures, he quickly devalues it by making the text (i.e., its words) function simply as "figures" and "signs" for events in the New Testament.

While the contribution of Hugh of St. Victor needs to be mentioned in this context lest it goes undervalued, Thomas Aquinas represents the formative personality in medieval era theological thought and, by extension, biblical hermeneutics. Aquinas marks a turning point in the understanding of the literal sense of the Scriptures as well as the conceptions of the reading of Scripture in general. He breaks with the Augustinian view of multiple levels of meaning in the text, both in terms of the categories and the source of multiplicity.[25] He creates a bigger distinction between the historical and literal senses of the text.[26] In Aquinas' thinking the historical means exactly what the words convey: "when something is proposed straightforwardly."[27] It is here that he sees the human authors at work, and their intentions emerge in the text at this point. His *sensus literalis* though consists of the meaning intended by the author of the text, God. And while he thinks that this meaning can be read on multiple levels like the "spiritual, plain and hidden, present and future,"[28] it contains one stable literal meaning. Aquinas, while open to the notion of multiplicity, views meaning in the text as being stable.

If Aquinas separates the historical and literal sense of Scripture, he also drives a wedge between the literal and spiritual. While agreeing with Augustine, Hugh of St. Victor, and Peter Lombard on the primacy of the literal sense of the Bible,[29] Aquinas elevates the literal sense over the spiritual, arguing that "in the sacred scripture . . . all the senses rest on a single one: the literal sense."[30] For Aquinas the literal sense lies not merely in the actual words of Scripture but in the intentions of God as author. In so doing Aquinas identifies a stable and single basis for apprehension of meaning that can lead to theological formulation.[31] The spiritual sense of Scripture he regards as too unstable for use in theological discourse, given that meanings change over time. Aquinas understands that the search for the spiritual sense of the text remains integral to the formation and practice of priests and monks, while the apprehension of the literal sense provides a basis for articulation of Christian faith and practice. In all of this, Aquinas does not conceive of the reading of the Scripture as a democratic exercise. Given the low levels of literacy, the foreignness of the Latin text, the technical skill required to read the Vulgate,[32] and the general ethos of who engages in reading the Bible, Aquinas develops his thinking to maintain current practices. In fact, his notion of the historical emphasizes the text and propels the study of the language, forms, grammar, and shape of texts—a complex skill even for that period. On the other hand, his notion of the literal as the divinely intended meaning through which one can glean the spiritual sense of the Scripture makes this into a highly developed spiritual practice suited to holy orders. On both levels Aquinas, his forebears, and contemporaries conceive of a select audience and readership of the Scriptures.

Some of the elements that would characterize Luther's position exist in the work of the interpreters just examined. James Preus views Luther as "radicalizing" tendencies in use at the time, "stretching, but not a breaking, of old forms."[33] The characterization of a Church that completely sets aside the Bible in preference for the human teaching of the *magesterium* oversimplifies the context of Luther's work. Luther reacts to the unity of the Church and the Scriptures accepted as a rule of faith during his time. From the time of the church fathers up to the sixteenth century, the interpretation of Scripture resides in the hands of the Pope.[34] Luther's argument that Scripture requires no interpreter because its plain sense communicates clear messages to the reader marks a departure from the norms of the time. He enters into practices of reading the Scripture that predate him and tweaks these to suit his hermeneutical lens. On the matter of the literal sense of the Bible, Luther is less the reformer, in the sense of redirecting some misguided notions, and more the innovator, in the sense of doing a new thing.

Luther walks the traditional path of interpreting Scripture by using the *quadriga,* but like Aquinas he prefers the literal sense. And, similar to Aquinas, he dismisses the notion of the multiple levels of meaning in Scripture.[35] As a monk and biblical scholar, Luther engages the Bible with the critical resources available at the time, including rigorous exegetical traditions. He shares in the knowledge and growth of knowledge about the texts of Scripture that come with the Scholastic movement's interest in discovering the Bible. To this extent, he holds views similar to Aquinas that the meaning of the text lies not behind the words but in the words themselves,[36] given that these words represent the intention of God. Therefore, the reading of Scripture serves as a spiritual practice that enables the reader to experience and hear God speaking through the Holy Spirit.

While Aquinas locates the literal sense of the Scripture in the divine intention, Luther identifies this as Christ. Preus recognizes Luther's christological exegesis and the equating of Christ as the literal sense of the Scriptures as definitive of Luther's contribution to the reading of the Scripture.[37] Up to this point, biblical exegesis derived christological content by way of figures, allegories, or types. Texts point to Christ or represent Christ in a symbolic or spiritual way, particularly the Old Testament. Luther shifts this and places Christ at the center of the Bible, not merely as a hermeneutical goal but as a literal presence in the words of the text.[38] In some ways he follows the example of Augustine who makes love a hermeneutical principle and touchstone for the Scriptures. And, like Augustine, he conceives of the presence of Christ in the Scripture in a deeply existential way, in the sense that an actual encounter takes place between the reader and Christ. Christ no longer appears as a concept on a page or thought in history or even a theological entity, but a living reality in the life of the reader or, better yet, the person of faith.

The notion of the literal in Luther stands not opposite the spiritual but rather as a preference for other terms like historical (*historicus*) or prophetic (*propheticus*).[39] He does not equate Christ with the historical or the prophetic since this places Christ in the past and locks Christ into a word or text or—put better—a "letter." History for him means words, or rather "word" for him means history and something past. Similarly, he views the prophetic as past and not available in the present. The divide between the literal and history that Aquinas opens up moves further apart in Luther. This does not mean that Luther disdains history or disregards the historical aspect of the texts.[40] In fact, he does pay attention to history so much that he collapses the distance between the history of the biblical world and the contemporary world.[41] In so doing, Luther argues for a straight line of interpretation from one world to the next without much inbetween.

Given his belief that the literal sense of the Scriptures lies in Christ, Luther maintains that the Scriptures remain plain and make sense as they stand for the most part. The Holy Spirit's role in authorship and its presentation of Christ to the reader requires no further clarity to get the sense of the Scriptures. Warning against the dangers of interpretation,[42] he maintains the clarity of Scriptures in a way that makes the Scriptures self-interpreting. But this clarity arises out of the content of the text and needs to be done following principles that do not produce contradictory or obscure meanings.[43] Although clarity of meaning exists in the text, Christ, Luther still holds the need for careful reading methods to ensure apprehension of the clear message. His preference for the literal makes sense in this regard, since to start with the allegorical or to rely unduly upon it disregards the direct object of God's Word, namely Christ. Therefore, the results of undue allegory stand as something other than the Word–word relationship that Luther constructs. This way he makes the Bible what David Lotz refers to as "self-authenticating . . . owing to its content."[44] Consequently, Luther marshals his academic resources to wrap the Scriptures in Christ with his equating of the literal with the grammatical.[45] In this fusing of the literal with the grammatical, Luther pays attention to the literal words on the page since they provide the deepest meaning of the text. As such he shuns the notion that the deepest meaning lies behind the words of the text in the way the later historical-critical methods would insist. In the actual words given in the text, the Holy Spirit opens the mind of the exegete to the meaning of the Scriptures, Christ. Robert Goeser speaks of this as the "incarnational use of language" that makes "Christ the 'scope' of Scripture. There is no literal meaning of Scripture apart from Christ."[46]

The construction that Luther effects results in a layered combination of what modern minds may regard as academic in one sense, spiritual in another, experiential in another sense, and existential. Since Christ is the Word that comes with the word, then faith stands as the goal of the Scriptures and their reading.[47] And if Christ stands as the literal sense of the Scriptures, then in reading them the person of faith, as distinct from the person of no faith or weak faith, should Luther make such distinctions, receives Christ. Lotz clarifies that in Luther's thinking "Christ proclaims himself in and through the gospel. . . . He 're-presents' himself everywhere today through this ongoing proclamation, even as he once 'presented' himself in the flesh in Palestine."[48] Lotz posits that a notion of the "real presence" with regard to the word can be developed in a similar way to the sacraments. Similarly, Goeser talks of Luther's notion that "God's Word is always attached to something created, something physical," and even though unseen comes to the person of faith as a "revelatory presence."[49] Luther's usage of *testimonia* and *meditatio* with regard to the hermeneutical and exegetical further reflects these ideas. He speaks of *testimonia* in the same way as God's promises but also as God's gift to human beings in the encounter with the Scriptures. Similarly, the art of exegesis compares with *meditatio* that opens up the inner being in the reading of Scriptures.[50] These categories and experiences exist within the confines of monastic life. Luther brings them to bear upon his reading practices and at the same time enjoins them to a wider audience. Supremely, he offers to this wider audience the experience of Christ in a literal way.

The modern oppositional categories of piety and learning do not hold together in Luther as separate entities that war against each other. Wolfhart Pannenberg shares that, for Luther, "theology [stands] as the object of intellectual inquiry and theology [shapes] . . . the sphere of a personal encounter, [together they form] an indivisible unity."[51] Theoretically, in Luther there appear the stirrings of a democraticizing of the Bible and an evangelical appeal for the Bible. Darrell Reinke believes that Luther speaks more as a "literate man" than "a Christian man,"[52] given the limitations of the printed text and literacy during his time. Even if Luther does not directly effect a program that places the Bible into the hands of all persons, he contributes ideas that clarify the Bible for readers whether they be members of monastic orders, priests, or academic teachers. Gerhard Ebeling offers that Luther in his lectures on the Psalms answers the concern of how to read the Scriptures, that it "speaks directly to the reader[s], affects [them] and comes to life in [their] heart[s]."[53] Summing up Luther's legacy on the literal sense as clarifying the Scriptures and enabling greater accessibility through and to its pages situates the way Luther appears in various guises in our contemporary religious scene. Luther's presence in the creation makes sense, as does his listing in the pantheon of personalities in the literalist movement. Oeming views Luther's contribution in the Reformation as consisting of his emphasis on the literal and his idea that the Bible is self-interpreting and, therefore, accessible.[54]

The history of the Church in many ways reflects its relationship with the Scriptures. Lotz offers that the encounter with the Bible defines Church history from a number of angles.[55] This history, for the most part, reflects the growing need to understand and read the Bible. It also demonstrates the increasing audience of readers and their desire to participate in a process that in the modern era includes more and more people with fewer technical skills. The appeal of the literal for the modern mind lies in its easy construction of reality and clear assertion of meaning. Yet addressing the need for clarity has never been a stumbling block for most hermeneutical and exegetical approaches, in fact this stirs and encourages them. The problem lies with those approaches that create further problems than they solve and in the process distort the meaning of the text.

The historical-critical approach, while a skilled exegetical method, remains unavailable to the unschooled, contributes to the distortion of the notion of the literal, and creates a crisis of interpretation. This method emerges in the nineteenth century and takes the focus off of the text as it exists at the time of the Medieval period and the Reformation and places it on the world behind the text. The drive to reconstruct events, communities of reception and tradition, histories, authors and their intentions results in the production of a solid historical world that lies behind the text. This historical world in time supersedes the text itself as it becomes the arbiter of meaning and interpretation for the text. Pannenberg raises the question as to whether the reconstructed history or the biblical texts should prove normative for theological construction.[56] The reality behind Pannenberg's question and the issues he raises appears to be the shrinking gap between the literal sense of the text and the historical.

The other spin-off of the historical-critical method in the articulation of a scientifically verified history behind the text lies in the construction of a reliable version of reality that resembles in a vague way the world of the reader.[57] The world behind the text no longer appears symbolic, imaginary, or even remote. Hans Frei explains the calculus this way: "'Meaning' is identical with 'possible truth,' and . . . if a story belongs to the genre of history-like or 'realistic' narrative, its meaning *qua* possible truth belongs to the class called 'factuality.'"[58] This then lies a short step away from rendering the words as factual and therefore ruling out any symbolic, allegorical content or even interpretation. It also permits the view that words mean exactly what they say and nothing else. The clarity principle reasserts itself in this formulation. However, unlike Luther where Christ makes the literal plain and the literal lies with Christ, the literal serves as the product not of faith, but of history.[59] Schneiders regards the equating of the historical with the literal as also closing the door to multiple meanings and stabilizing interpretation for all time.[60] Therefore, the literal notions only require that a bridge be built from the ancient world to the present to ensure the passage of the original message.

This trans-historical passage masks the abstractions that occur in reading the Bible and pretends to be a tactile process. Though it results in tangible benefits for readers, it stands no less in the mold of rarefied concepts seeking to become reality in the lives of readers. Several interpreters have made this move. Augustine relies on the virtues of love to make his Bible come alive. Aquinas leaves it to divine intention to determine textual meaning. Luther locates Christ at his hermeneutical center. The historical-critical method relies upon reconstructed history to create meaning. And, similarly, modern literalists stand upon a concept of "biblical history" to serve their reading of the Bible. The act of Bible reading involves several moves from abstraction to reality, from distance to proximity. The variable factor, interestingly, is not the biblical texts but the rarefied hermeneutical principle employed. At various stages this principle has been called "literal." As a moveable concept, the literal, therefore, can be reinterpreted and redefined to serve contemporary readers' desire for access and proximity to the Bible. Recasting the literal sense of the text as located in the community of readers rather than in the plain words of the text can be one way to redefine the concept.

For most of history, meaning inheres in the text of the Bible, and readers with varying degrees of skill comb through the pages to discover the nuggets of truth planted there. These nuggets lay there either intentionally hidden by a divine and/or human author, and/or they intentionally or otherwise lay exposed for all to see their wares. Much postmodern reading theory assigns meaning outside of texts. In the writings of some biblical scholars, though, a willingness exists to probe the idea that the Bible's meaning lies not in the pages awaiting an epochal event or the right levels of faith to confront the reader, but outside in the reader and the reading community. Schneiders rationalizes that theological exegesis, with its aim to identify a literal meaning that equates with authorial intention, already brings meaning from outside of the Bible to its construction of meaning.[61] She suggests that theological positions add and shape whatever the exegete unearths as the divine or human authorial intention. Given that theological exegesis uncritically expands the notion of the literal, room exists for a broadening of the conception of the literal in modern reading communities. With Hans Gadamer she views the text as a mediator of meaning that possesses excess of meaning. This meaning comes forth in the reading encounter: "The understanding of the reader is, in other words, constitutive (although not exclusively so) of the meaning of the text."[62] Effectively, Schneiders advocates for the work of theological exegesis on a more conscious level by non-experts.

In a similar way, Hans Frei goes outside of the text into the reading community to locate the literal sense of the reading of Scripture. While not offering to democratize the construction of meaning as Schneiders, Frei believes that the faith community forms the descriptive center out of which the literal sense of the Bible emerges. He leans more towards the faith aspect of the community rather than towards the everydayness of the community. He sees the religious dimensions of "beliefs, ritual, and behavior patterns, ethos as well as narrative"[63] forming the dimensions that mark the community as well as contributing to the reading posture. Like Schneiders, who does not completely hand over meaning to the reader, Frei also keeps meaning within the boundaries of faith and theological forms. Loughlin, who uses Frei's ideas, expands Frei's notion of the faith community to define the Church within its contemporary context. In doing so a literal meaning emerges for the Church community as it exists within the "circumstances of its time and place."[64] For him the reading encounter transforms the reading community as it adjusts its vision and self-identity to "the one whom the Scripture depicts."[65] Loughlin stands in the mold of Luther who assigns existential qualities to the act of reading the Scriptures and, while he makes no identification of Christ as the center of the Scriptures, Loughlin understands it to command a compelling quality enough to call communities to enact the visions they unearth in its reading. In this regard, he holds stronger to the Bible than does Schneiders or Frei.

In laying out a new understanding of the *sensus literalis*, locating the literal sense in the community of readers seems plausible from at least three perspectives. However, pushing this beyond the simple acknowledgment of the community of readers to defining the community in its fullest expression as the descriptive location of the literal becomes necessary. This means, first of all, not limiting the community of readers to possession of faith as the sole requirement for bringing meaning to the text; although this may be foundational in some instances, it ought not to be determinative. While confessional and theological commitments should never be eliminated in the reading of the Bible, they are not the only framers of surplus meaning worthy of attention. Secondly, the emphasis on the community in its fullest expression pays attention to the everydayness of the community. As Frei and Loughlin speak of the community of readers, they work within the boundaries of faith and worship. However, the commitments of Church and worship not only shape people in their existence, but numerous interactions in their everyday lives impact their sense of self and identity. That these too should be taken seriously in constituting the fullness of the reading community needs to be stressed to avoid placing filters on aspects of the lives of the community that can or cannot be valid for reading the Bible. Then, thirdly, the emphasis on the literal being the expression of the reading community at its fullest speaks to the community at it is presently constituted and what it can become. This becoming may not reflect the narratives and descriptions of the Bible in Loughlin's categories as well as it may, but it forms part of the identity of the reading community that constantly re-forms itself and brings new insight into the reading of the Bible. It also leaves room for the existential encounter that Luther believes happens in the moment of reading the Scriptures.

The stress on the community of readers as the source for the construction of the literal sense of the Scriptures reflects the progressive shift in modern Bible reading strategies. Equally, it places responsibility for meaning into the hand of ordinary readers and invites their participation in the construction of meaning. A. K. M. Adam offers that the invitation acknowledges that "people interpret constantly and so successfully."[66] Similarly, Gerald West steps back from using the word "educate" in preference for "sharing the resources of biblical scholarship" with regard to his approach to reading "with" the poor and marginalized since it presumes that they bring nothing to the table. He insists that interpretive resources already exist in the reading community for reading the Bible.[67] They both speak to the democratizing of the reading process beyond the boundaries as conceived by Luther and the Reformers that result in the dismantling of hierarchies of interpretation. More importantly, they enable the vernacular, the language of the ordinary and the everyday, to enter into the encounter with the text. Rather than desacralizing the text of Scripture, this re-sacralizes it through the entry of the lives of reading communities into an experience outside of their own in a way that they then add to their everyday lives the insight and discoveries of the numinous and the external that they will then call sacred.

The principles outlined here grow out of the reading quadrant that locates the reader at the center of the reading process.[68] They advocate the abandonment of the search for the literal inside of the text, in the past or even in the theological constructions of the Church. Locating the literal within the community of readers and flattening though not eliminating the hierarchies of interpretation shifts meaning away from an exclusive lock in the past, opens it in the present, and opens up the reading community to the future. This enables what D. Christopher Spinks regards as the transcendent in the act of reading the Scriptures—the coincidence of past, present, and future.[69] Reading communities rather than just merely the text participate in the trans-historical events that create meaning in the present. These communities read with the past as much as with their future, and they get to experience these poles and receive opportunities to grow into greater fullness. Should this happen as a result of the encounter with the Scriptures, then truly it deserves the descriptor "Book of Faith."

## Endnotes

[1] See http://www.answersingenesis.org/creation/v6/i3/luther.asp. Accessed on 02/06/2009.

[2] By this I mean here those who hold to the major tenets of the nineteenth century fundamentalist movement, particularly the notion of biblical inerrancy.

[3] Sung by the Statler Brothers.

[4] The medieval Jewish exegete Rabbi Solomon bar Isaac (commonly known as "RaShI"), focused attention on the literal meaning of texts (*peshat*) and moved

away from the common reliance upon the ethical and legendary method (*derash*) in much the same way Luther would later do. Rashi's impact upon Luther comes via Nicholas de Lyre whose work liberally quotes Rashi and had become standard reading for Christian scholars and orders in the Medieval period. The impact of Rashi's thought upon Luther is acknowledged in the rhyme, "If Lyra had not played, Luther would not have danced." Jacob Rader Marcus, *The Jew in the Medieval World: A Source Book 315 – 1791* (Cincinnati: Hebrew Union College Press, 2000), 412. Ronald S. Hendel, "The Plain Sense of Scripture: Do You Recognize it When You See It," *Bible Review* 13 (1997): 17.

5  Sandra Schneiders shows how critical exegetes like Krister Stendhal and John McKenzie argue that the task of exegesis lies in discovering the intended meaning of the author and not in interpretations. She concludes that this position asserts "the literal meaning of the text is perfectly stable and univocal, and its meaning in the past is its only meaning." Sandra M. Schneiders, "Faith, Hermeneutics, and the Literal Sense of Scripture." *Theological Studies* 39 (1978): 722.

6  Schneiders observes that for "the ordinary reader 'really' means 'literally,'" Schneiders, 720. In the same vein Stephen Fowl sees the modern conception of literal as "having only one meaning." Stephen E. Fowl, "The Importance of a Multivoiced Literal Sense of Scripture: The Example of Thomas Aquinas" in *Reading Scripture with the Church: Toward a Hermeneutic for Theological Interpretation*, ed. A. K. M. Adam; Stephen E. Fowl, Kevin J. Vanhoozer, Francis Watson (Grand Rapids, Michigan: Baker Academic, 2006), 35.

7  The early ascetic John Cassian developed the *quadriga*. Mark D. Thompson, *A Sure Ground on Which to Stand: The Relation of Authority and Interpretive Method in Luther's Approach to Scripture* (Cumbria, Great Britain: Paternoster, 2004), 27.

8  Admittedly, the influence of Greco-Roman literary and philosophical traditions already can be seen in several New Testament texts and the way their writers approach the Old Testament as their scripture. For example, Paul sees Hagar and Sarah as types in his writing in Galatians, and he writes about the law using allegories of trees, athletics, and grafting in Romans. The conception in the Gospel of Matthew that the life of Jesus fulfils predictions and statements in prophecy represents the full flowering of the allegory stated in these earlier texts. In effect, meanings and positions that the writers of the Genesis texts never envisaged are laid upon the texts in a way that make this not simply a way to read them but their spiritual and original meaning.

9  Kenneth Hagen uses the term "grammar of faith" to argue for a uniqueness of the biblical texts that requires special reading approaches. I do not believe that the New Testament writings are that unique in terms of their writing conventions and genres, perhaps with the exception of the forms of the gospels as biographies and the apocalypse, as compared with literature produced in their contemporary context. Hagan, though, is more concerned about revelation and reception of divine revelation by means of texts than with actual human language. As an ethereal reality this would be difficult to capture in a systematic approach to reading texts. Kenneth Hagen. *Luther's Approach to Scripture as seen in his 'Commentaries' on Galatians 1519-1538* (Tübingen: J.C.B. Mohr [Paul Siebeck], 1993), 47.

10. Manfred Oeming, *Contemporary Biblical Hermeneutics: An Introduction*, trans. Joachim Vette (Great Britain: Ashgate, 2006), 9.

11. Both Philo and Origen share similar commitments in their approach to sacred texts. They both understand the role of human agency in the writing of texts but regard the divine agency as supreme. As such they resort to the use of allegory since they accept that human language remains capable of distorting the divine message and that the allegorical method provides a fix of some sort to apprehend the real meaning intended by God. William Yarchin, *History of Biblical Interpretation: A Reader* (Peabody, Massachusetts: Hendrickson, 2004), 18-41.

12. James Preus maintains that the Church's response of allegory and typology to the issues of dualism raised by Marcion not only proves the validity of Marcion's ideas but also defines allegory as the essential way to read the texts. James Samuel Preus, *From Shadow to Promise: Old Testament Interpretation from Augustine to the Young Luther* (Cambridge, Massachusetts: Harvard University Press, 1969), 10. Similarly, Oeming argues that Platonic ideals influence the later decision of the Church to retain the Old Testament as part of the Bible. Oeming, 11.

13. Thompson, 25. Yarchin, 42.

14. Thompson, 44.

15. Oeming, 10. Thompson credits Aristotle as having the larger impact, especially upon Aquinas. Thompson, 44.

16. Preus cites Augustine as an ardent supporter of the unity of the Bible to withstand the Manichean teachings. Preus, 10.

17. Thompson, 26.

18. He defines further a doubled reality of love as in the gospels as love of God and neighbor.

19. Preus, 13.

20. Tyconius holds this view of the texts as "oracular" and therefore mysterious, requiring rules for interpretation. Luther draws upon his lists in some ways but backs off their usage and his "rules" terminology. Yarhin, 51.

21. Yarchin, xii.

22. In a commentary on Genesis, Bede inveighs against the excessive use of allegory to the detriment of the historical sense, arguing that the faith is tied to the historical sense of the text. Thompson, 38.

23. Pannenberg traces the notion of the literal sense of Scripture back to Hugh of St. Victor. Wolfhart Pannenberg, *Basic Questions in Theology*, Vol. 1, trans. George H. Kehm (Philadelphia: Fortress Press, 1970), 4.

24. Preus, 35. Peter Lombard holds similarly views but adds greater numbers of dialectics like law/grace, letter/spirit. Preus, 38.

25. Aquinas thinks that the literal sense of Scripture reflects the intentions of God as author. This leads him to believe that verses of Scripture can contain "many literal senses." Fowl, 45. Hence, "since it is the literal sense which the author intends, and since the author is God, who comprehends all things in his mind together,

'it is not unfitting that there should literally be several interpretations contained in one scriptural word.'" Thomas Aquinas, *Summa Theologiae* I, 1-13. Tr. with Commentary by Brian J. Shanley (Indianapolis: Hackett Publishing, 2006), 17. The distinction between this position and the multiple levels of meaning of Augustine lies in that fact that for Augustine and others the use of the *quadriga* produces these different levels, while for Aquinas multiplicity, when it exists, results from divine causation.

[26] Aquinas cites Augustine's categories of the levels of meanings in a text as historical, aetiological, and allegorical, but then adds parabolic to the lists. He refines the list by speaking of the three spiritual senses as allegorical, moral, and anagogical. Then he elevates the literal above all else and separates it from the historical by speaking of history, aetiology, and anagogy as pertaining to "the same literal sense." Aquinas, 17.

[27] Aquinas, 17.

[28] Preus, 54.

[29] Thompson, 39.

[30] Aquinas, 17.

[31] Aquinas appears ambiguous on the matter of multiplicity as he balances this notion on the necessity for clarity in the Scriptures. He writes: "A multiplication of senses in one scriptural passage produces confusion and deception, and it undermines an argument's firmness; and so the multiplication of premises does not result in a sound argument but rather leads to a number of fallacies. . . . Thus a scripture passage ought not communicate multiple senses." Aquinas, 15. Wood offers that the Middle Ages sees the development of the literal sense of the text as the source for theological disputations and exegesis but playing no part in the normative fourfold meaning of the text. A. Skevington Wood, *Luther's Principles of Biblical Interpretation* (London: Tyndale Press, 1960), 24.

[32] Thompson asserts that even if one could read Latin, the liberties taken in the Vulgate with Latin make it difficult for the ordinary reader. Thompson, 34.

[33] Preus, 154.

[34] Hermann Sasse, "Luther and the Word of God" in *Accents in Luther's Theology: Essays in Commemoration of the 450th Anniversary of the Reformation*, ed. Heino O. Kadai. (St. Louis: Concordia Publishing House, 1967), 57. Pannenberg observes that Luther's position on this issue is not the first instance of resistance to the notion. He cites the case of William of Ockham in the fourteenth century who deals with the priority of the interpreted Scripture in relation to the teaching office. Pannenberg, 5.

[35] Oeming, 14. Hagen, 17.

[36] Sasse, 70.

[37] Preus, 20

[38] Luther describes the Bible as "the swaddling clothes and the manger in which Christ lies. . . . Simple and lowly are these swaddling clothes, but dear is the treasure, Christ who lies in them," *Luthers Works* 35:236.

39 Preus, 44.

40 Luther takes Origen and Jerome to task for "depart[ing] from the historical account, which they call 'the letter that kills' and 'the flesh'; and they bestow lofty praise on the 'spiritual meaning,' of which they have no actual knowledge," *Luther's Works* 1:231.

41 Admittedly, the notion of the historical distance between the worlds from a hermeneutical sense is not well grasped at that time, even though some humanists conceive of the idea and the problem it poses. Hagen, 32.

42 Hagen, 17.

43 Pannenberg, 5.

44 David W. Lotz, "Sola Scriptura: Luther on Biblical Authority" *Interpretation* 35 (1981), 268, note 30.

45 Sasse, 70.

46 Robert J. Goeser, "Luther and the Heart's Native Language" (lecture presented at the Graduate Theological Union Distinguished Faculty Lecture, Berkeley, California, November 1981), 9.

47 Preus, 189.

48 Lotz, 271.

49 Robert J. Goeser, "The Doctrine of Word and Scripture in Luther and Lutheranism" in *The Report of the Lutheran-Episcopal Dialogue,* Second Series 1976-1980. (Cincinnati: Forward Movement, 1981), 120.

50 Darrell R. Reinke, "From Allegory to Metaphor: More Notes on Luther's Hermeneutical Shift." *Harvard Theological Review* 66 (1973), 389.

51 Pannenberg, 95.

52 Reinke, 395.

53 Gerhard Ebeling. *Luther: An Introduction to His Thought*, trans. R. A. Wilson (Philadelphia: Fortress Press, 1980), 110.

54 Oeming, 14.

55 Lotz, 258.

56 Pannenberg, 7. Of course, he observes that in the quest to provide clarity on the Bible, the historical-critical method renders itself into a highly complex set of functions requiring technical skill. The tools to reconstruct each historical moment or to define the world that creates specific texts are not readily available to most readers. Gerhard Ebeling confronts a similar set of questions in *The Problem of Historicity: In the Church and its Proclamation,* tr. Grover Foley (Philadelphia: Fortress Press, 1967).

57 Loughlin offers that the modern conception of the literal only requires that the history reconstructed not be "figural" but scientifically verifiable. The historical-critical method provides this. Gerard Loughlin, "Following to the Letter: The Literal Use of Scripture." *Literature and Theology* 9 (1995), 375.

[58] Frei, 62. Loughlin posits that the relationship between the historical and the literal in the modern period stands further apart than it has in history. In this regard, he makes the distinction between the literal as history and the literal as written and uses the neologism "letteral" to describe the modern idea of the literal as written. Loughlin, 372.

[59] On this point the proponents of modern literalist views that compress text and history cite Luther's dismissal of allegory as mere "decorations" as conclusive evidence that he rejected the allegorical method. Both the preface to his *Lectures on Psalms* and his treatment of the Psalms demonstrate Luther's continued use of the allegorical approach. In the preface he lays out how the *quadriga* works with respect to place names like Jerusalem or Babylon. He also asserts, "One indeed takes in an allegorical sense only what is elsewhere stated historically." *Luther's Works: First Lectures on the Psalms* I, ed. Hilton C. Oswald. (St. Louis: Concordia Publishing House, 1974), 4.

[60] Schneiders, 722. Schneiders observes that even with Robert Grant, who embraces the thinking of "presuppositionless understandings" and makes room for multiplicity in interpretation, he falls back to the position that exegesis discovers the one intended original message.

[61] Schneiders, 728.

[62] Schneiders, 731.

[63] Frei, 70.

[64] Loughlin, 379.

[65] Loughlin, 370.

[66] A. K. M. Adam. *Faithful Interpretation: Reading the Bible in a Postmodern World* (Minneapolis: Fortress Press, 2006), 91.

[67] Gerald O. West, "Reading Other-Wise: Socially Engaged Biblical Scholars Reading with Their Local Communities: An Introduction" in *Reading Other-Wise: Socially Engaged Biblical Scholars Reading with Their Local Communities,* ed. Gerald O. West (Atlanta: Society of Biblical Literature, 2007), 2.

[68] The loyalties described here reflect those that may be found in base communities in Latin America during the heyday of liberation theology. They coincide with the feminist, African-American, postcolonial, *meujerista*, Native American, Asian, or any ethnically-based biblical hermeneutics.

[69] D. Christopher Spinks, *The Bible and the Crisis of Meaning: Debates on the Theological Interpretation of Scripture* (London: T&T Clark, 2007), 19.

# The Lecturers

## Craig L. Nessan

Craig L. Nessan is Academic Dean and Professor of Contextual Theology at Wartburg Theological Seminary in Dubuque, Iowa. He teaches courses in the areas of contextual theology, pastoral theology, and theological ethics. He has oversight of the seminary's internship program.

Dr. Nessan has served eleven years as a parish pastor in Philadelphia, Pennsylvania, and Cape Girardeau, Missouri. He holds degrees from Michigan State University, Wartburg Theological Seminary, and the University of Munich. His theological interests include ecclesiology, theological ethics, liberation theology, and family systems theory.

## Mark Allan Powell

Mark Allan Powell is the Robert and Phyllis Leatherman Professor of New Testament at Trinity Lutheran Seminary, Columbus, Ohio.

Dr. Powell has a B.A. from Texas Lutheran College, an M.Div. from Trinity Lutheran Seminary, and earned his Ph.D. from Union Theological Seminary. He has served pastorates in Pasadena, Texas, 1980-84, and Richmond, Virginia, 1984-86. He has been Assistant Professor of New Testament, Trinity Seminary, 1987-92; Director of Continuing Education and Post-Graduate Studies, Trinity Seminary, 1989-92; Associate Professor of New Testament, Trinity Seminary, 1992-97; Robert and Phyllis Leatherman Professor of New Testament, Trinity Seminary, 1998-.

## Esther Menn

Esther Menn, is the Marilyn and Ralph Klein Chair of Old Testament Studies, Professor of Old Testament and Director of Advanced Studies, Lutheran School of Theology at Chicago.. She joined the faculty of her alma mater (M.A., 1985) in the 2001-02 academic year.

Dr. Menn taught previously in the department of religious studies at the University of Virginia (1995-2001), where she was promoted to associate rank and granted tenure in 2001. While at the University of Virginia, she spent a sabbatical year as a visiting scholar at Hebrew University of Jerusalem and a W. F. Albright associate fellow, supported by an American Council of Learned Societies Fellowship. She has been an adjunct faculty member at McCormick Theology Seminary (1995), a lecturer at the University of Chicago Divinity School (1994-95, 2004-06), and instructor at California Lutheran University Department of Religion (1988-90).

At LSTC Menn teaches courses in Old Testament, organizes events and conferences in Jewish-Christian relations, and oversees the Th.M. and Ph.D. programs as Director of Advanced Studies.

## Mary Hinkle Shore

Mary Hinkle Shore is Professor of New Testament, Luther Seminary. She joined the Luther Seminary faculty as Assistant Professor of New Testament in the fall of 1997.

Dr. Shore received the B.A. degree *summa cum laude* from Capital University in Columbus, Ohio, in 1982. In 1986 she graduated from Luther Northwestern Theological Seminary, and was ordained in the Evangelical Lutheran Church in America. Following ordination she served for six years in rural and suburban parish settings in North Dakota.

She earned the Ph.D. degree in New Testament and Christian Origins from Duke University in 1997. While at Duke, she was a teaching assistant in undergraduate religion courses, as well as a preceptor for New Testament and homiletics courses in the Divinity School.

## Steed Vernyl Davidson

Steed Vernyl Davidson is Assistant Professor of Old Testament at Pacific Lutheran Theological Seminary.

Dr. Davidson has B.A. and a M.A. from the University of the West Indies; his S.T.M. is from Boston University, his M.Phil. from Union Theological Seminary, and his Ph.D. from Union Theological Seminary

He has served as pastor of United Methodist congregations in New York and the Caribbean; as Instructor, Union Theological Seminary in the City of New York; as Visiting Assistant Professor of Religion, Luther College, Decorah, Iowa. He has been at Pacific Lutheran Theological Seminary since 2007.